The Beginner's Guide to Japan

JM Hewitt

To Masami, for all the years

Table of Contents

Introduction

The origins of today, a very brief history of Japan

In 1600, after centuries of war, Japan was united at the Battle of Sekigahara under a single Shogun, Tokugawa Ieyasu, ushering in the start of the Edo Period. What followed was two hundred and fifty years of peace and self-imposed isolation, the complete disarmament of guns from the country and then the arrival in 1853 of the Black Ships under Admiral Perry. At this point Japan embarked on the path of modernization with the rapid opening of a feudal society to international influences, a civil war in 1868 that saw the overthrow of the still ruling Tokugawa Shogunate, and transfer of power to the Emperor with the beginning of the Meiji Restoration.

The sinking of the Russian fleet in 1904, the first victory by an Asian power over a great European one, led to further rapid militarization and then, over the next few decades, there transpired a slight disagreement with most of the rest of the world. In 1945 the Emperor renounced his divinity, taking one final sip of tea as he did so, and from that time onwards Japan has been again at peace, working to rebuild a shattered nation, seeing massive growth and modernization and by the 1960s becoming the second largest economy on Earth. Under the protective umbrella of an American security treaty, *today Japan is threatened only by acts of God*. And those can be managed.

A little light background on Japan

At first sight Tokyo is part of Japan, there is only one way to count, time is simply time and isn't needed to say hello, your bank account can't be emptied with a small piece of wood the size of your thumb and you'd rather be approximately right than precisely wrong. In this book I look at some of the common questions people raise and some of the differences between Japan and other societies. This first section goes into these preconceptions and raises some of the key differences between that which travellers to Japan have been used to most of their lives and that which you are about to experience.

I came to Japan for two years in the early nineties and haven't quite got around to leaving yet. It's been a continuously enjoyable and rewarding experience and I've probably made every single gaijin faux pas there is to make and had some very kind and patient friends to help me find my way. This book is a collection of my experiences in Japan from my time here and the learnings of being in a society where *there are no right or wrongs compared to your home country. Just differences.* And there is always something new to learn.

When I started working here, I received some excellent advice from an old Japan hand. He told me to change myself, it would be a lot faster than trying to change Japan. At the time I didn't completely comprehend the meaning or the importance of what he was telling me. In hindsight these were very wise words! Some twenty years later I remain grateful for this advice as it has helped me enjoy my time here all the more.

He was right, *there are 127 million Japanese people who are used to a certain way; there's one of you and sometimes you're going to need to change.* The alternative is a constant stream of unending frustration and missed opportunity becoming hung up on even minor difficulties. Japan may not be your home country, but it is a wonderful place to live. Change when you have to and enjoy it all the more.

Some travellers arrive in Japan and see the wonders of a new world. Others arrive like they have just landed on Mars. This book has been written to take some of the mystery out of living in Japan and help those on their way, as well as the newly arrived, find their bearings more quickly. Although having been in Japan over twenty years, I would put myself in the class of "still learning every day" and although have experienced much so far, it only goes to illustrate how much more I have to go.

Japan is a wonderful experience whether you are simply travelling or moving to the country for an extended period of time. There are a myriad of guidebooks recommending places to go and things to try. This book doesn't aim to compete with those, this is a simple introduction to something very different from your previous experiences. Yes, all the people that said it were right, *Japan is different.*

Perhaps your company has just informed you that you're about to be posted to Japan for the next two years. Alternatively, you've decided to try English teaching in a country essentially new to you. This book has been written to explain the many seemingly incomprehensible situations you find yourself in.

Japanese people are invariably polite and helpful whatever the situation. I remember taking my parents to dinner one night many years ago and, as we drove through central Tokyo at the end of the evening, a group of teenagers ran across the road in front of our taxi seemingly oblivious to the world around them but causing our taxi to suddenly brake. Much to my amazement, when they reached the other side of the road, they all stopped, turned round and bowed in apology for having inconvenienced our journey. It has to be said, you wouldn't see that in many other countries.

Is it really different? – the question

Yes! I had been in Japan for a while when I was with some friends at their apartment in south Osaka on a quiet Saturday evening. We decided to have pizza and, given that my friends spoke no Japanese at all, I was volunteered as the least worst speaker for the task of calling the pizza delivery number. Asking my friends how they usually coped with this as it obviously wasn't their first pizza, they explained they would call the number, repeat the order several times and then hang up. Thirty minutes later their pizza would arrive. "Simple" they said.

So I called the number and asked to place an order. The voice at the other end let out a cry and said the equivalent of "Thank god! Someone who speaks Japanese. Can you tell them this isn't the pizza restaurant, they've been calling the wrong number for months and we've been taking the order and passing it on!"

As far as my friends were concerned there had been nothing wrong as thirty minutes after they'd ordered, their pizza would always arrive. Each time, the family had received their call and diligently taken the order before forwarding it on to the pizza place.

After we stopped laughing (and the Japanese family had also seen the amusing side of this) it took a while for this to sink in; nowhere else in the world would people ever be kind enough to do this, nowhere else in the world would someone have a story similar to this. Japan really was different.

You will often hear from people who have lived in Japan that it is different from anywhere they've experienced before and if in business, you'll soon find yourself explaining to your head office in your home country "but it's different here". The origin of this is that things really do work in a different way in Japan. *There's no wrong or right about it, it's just different.*

The key question is "what does *different* actually mean?" This is the sixty-four thousand dollar question. "Different" in this context relates to not simply the differences of the physical world around us but to the way people think and relate themselves to a society, their expectations and the expectations of others on them. The relation to authority or seniority and the question of what is wrong and what is right can be diametrically opposite to a foreigner's experience and how form can sometimes be more important than substance. The list is, to all intents and purposes, unending. Everything you thought you knew is essentially no longer relevant, a somewhat liberating experience.

Over the years, one of my roles has evolved to be the bridge between the Japanese approach and the Western style of thinking. One of the most difficult situations is when a new foreigner to Japan thinks, and genuinely believes, that they either understand Japan or that their experiences in their home country should define their approach to Japan. There is nothing more uninformed in business than a foreigner who thinks they understand. A healthy viewpoint is to accept that everything may be a new experience and approach each new situation with an open mind. When you arrive at Narita airport don't assume that the Japanese words above the English sign that says "Welcome to Japan" are the Japanese version of the same message. *They aren't, they say "Welcome Home".*

Is Tokyo Japanese?

Tokyo is one of the world's great international cities, in some ways more so that London or New York. However, although quintessentially Japanese, once you are outside Tokyo, you are genuinely in a different world. I have friends who have lived in Tokyo for more than twenty years with effectively no Japanese language ability and can still simply direct taxis and order pizza. This is possible in Tokyo (though it could be argued that life might be easier with just a little more language) and it's quite possible to live and work here without any broad understanding of language, spoken or written.

Once outside Tokyo the English signs disappear very quickly and people are much less used to seeing foreigners. When I first arrived I lived in Osaka, a magnificent but ultimately domestic city. Small kids used to run up and touch me and run off laughing that they'd touched a foreigner. I once had an entire class of schoolchildren line up in front of me on a train and, in turn, asked me to sign their school notebook, as they'd never met a foreigner before. In Tokyo, we're effectively yesterday's news.

So, if you're up for an adventure, book a Shinkansen ticket to somewhere you haven't heard of, perhaps towards the Japan sea coast, and enjoy a few days re-learning sign language and getting to know a delightful, though somewhat hidden, aspect of Japan. Living in Tokyo is a remarkable metropolitan experience but Tokyo is a very different reflection of Japan than anything outside the capital.

Two nationalities – "Japanese" and "Foreigner"

Japan has a very straightforward approach to the question of nationality in everyday life. There are simply two nationalities, "Japanese", and "Foreign". Traditionally no distinction is made as to where a non-Japanese person came from, they are simply foreign. The word "gaijin", the word used as reference to any non-Japanese person, means literally "outside person". This is used in everyday conversation however the slightly more polite "gaikokujin" – a "person from an outside country", would be used on television or in the newspapers but the distinction of two nationalities remains.

Throughout this text you will see me refer to foreigner and, although I place emphasis on Western practices at certain points, we are all, simply, foreigners. The origins of the word date to the Meiji era when the government standardized a number of terms in use at the time including "strange people" and "the people with red hair". However, the importance of the description goes significantly beyond simple vocabulary and is more a way of life and thinking and this is the reason why, throughout this book, I adopt the Japanese style and refer to Japanese, and foreigners rather than individual nationalities.

Numbers – if you are flat or round

There is more than one way to count in Japan. Many more. A simple one, two, three, four, five, can be ichi, ni, san, shi, go or it can also be hitotsu, futatsu, mitsu, yotsu, itsustu, depending on what you are actually counting or the context within which you are speaking. If you focus on the first system you are on safer ground, however you may not be technically correct.

Added to the difference in the way numbers are counted are the systems applied for counting objects. There are, in fact, thirty-six different numbering systems in general use in Japan depending on the shape, size or type of item being counted. A flat item would be counted as "ichimai" – one flat item, where as a drinking glass would be counted as "ippai" – one open container shaped item and a bottle would "ippon" – one closed contained shaped item. Note how the suffix changes in each case dependent on the object itself.

However, there is then an added complication on top of this. The pronunciation of the suffix will change in a rotating set of three. Thus, when, for example, ordering bottles of wine, rather than being "ippon", "nippon", "sanpon" for one, two and three bottles of wine, one bottle is "ippon", two bottles are "nihon" and three bottles are "sanbon". This rotation of suffix is applicable to all counting systems so, in this instance, it may seem superfluous, however, telling the time can become complex when you need to apply the correct ending for which minute it is as well as the suffix for minutes generally.

Animals can be counted in two different systems depending on their size so one small dog would be "ippiki" where as a cow would be "itto". The cut off point for this seems to be around the size of a Labrador, above which all animals are counted with the "-to" suffix and below which they are counted with "-piki". Based on discussions with Japanese friends over the years, there is general disagreement over how to count Labradors by the way.

Airplanes, typhoons, children, all have their own counting systems and I have had the experience of a blank stare in the post office when asking for three stamps but using the suffix for machinery and the person behind the counter being at a total loss for what this foreigner was asking for.

Some of the issues around this can be alleviated by using your fingers to count out a number. However, whereas in the West numbers are counted as the fingers on one hand first followed by the second hand, held open and separately, when the number exceeds five, in Japan, numbers over five are indicated by holding the first hand completely open and the additional number of digits being held against the palm of the first hand. For example, seven would be indicated by holding the left hand completely open and holding the index and middle finger of the right hand against the palm of the left. People tend to do this very quickly so you need to be watching, however it's a very simple way to confirm the floor you need to get off in an elevator when you're visiting someone in a new building.

The other issue about counting in Japan that takes a little getting used to is that, whereas in the West, the counting system is based on units of a thousand, in Japan they are based on units of ten thousand. You are most likely to encounter difficulties with this when taking money out of a bank ATM. You may expect that you're trying to take out ¥30,000 but you've actually just ordered ¥300,000 (or more to the point, ¥30,0000).

As a result of this, if you are looking for a reasonably priced apartment, always remember to add another zero to the numbers you're reading, it may not be quite the bargain you anticipated.

The system works as follows:

"One thousand" is the same in Japanese "one thousand"
"Ten thousand" is stated as "one ten-thousand"
"One million" is then "one-hundred ten-thousands"

One area where this can cause particular problems is during translation. The numbering system is so ingrained into everyone that it is very easy for a translator to miss the change in the base counting system even when they're very experienced and focused on this as an issue. If the numbers don't feel right to you, always double-check and confirm, it's better than having a surprise later and usually everyone in the room will see the amusing side of what could have quite easily gone very wrong.

As Japan is in Asia, is it really that different?

One of the pleasures of moving to a new country is literally that you are moving to a new country. Japan, as is true for all countries, has many aspects unique to the culture and population. Although historically influenced by other Asian countries, most notably China through the introduction of a written language and more recently America through several decades of close cooperation, Japan is a blend of all with the addition of its own originality.

Countries and cultures are different, as are the way of business, the lifestyle, social structure, philosophies and so on. The learnings from one may be relevant to another but are unlikely to be directly associated. Japanese is a unique language as are elements of the written language in hiragana and katakana. The experiences gained in one Asian country are therefore unlikely to be directly applicable to the necessities of life in Japan. The answer to the question, is Japan really different to other Asian countries, is then, yes, it really is.

A time dependent approach to saying "hello"

This may sound strange but there genuinely isn't a direct translation of a simple "hello" in Japanese. If you ask a Japanese colleague though, the answer will probably be "konnichi-ha" (pronounced "konnichi-wa" but written "-ha"). However this is closer akin to "good day". In the mornings you can use "ohaiyo gozaimasu" but you'd risk chuckles if you used konnichi-wa before 10.00am. The general guideline goes like this:

Ohaiyo gozaimasu is equivalent to "good morning"

Konnichi-wa equals "good day" and is used until sunset

Konban-wa is then "good evening" and used during the night.

As I say, there really is no direct translation of hello. And nothing wrong with that if you think in English it was only adopted widely with the introduction of the telephone.

Sightseeing in Tokyo – doesn't take too long

This, not being a guidebook, will be a short section. There are many helpful guidebooks about Japan, however, what many fail to mention is that Tokyo is a city where there is a lot to do, many places to go, but not actually very much to see. You can take a bus ride in English around the city, though a full day will cover pretty much everything there is to photograph.

This is especially true for the trip to the Imperial Palace. You will get to see the gate, a lot of tourists, both foreign and Japanese, and that's about it. There used to be no buildings high enough in the area to allow the public to see the Palace itself but in the early 2000s new buildings in the Hibiya district opened restaurants from where you can see into the home of the Emperor. And in reality it's not all that interesting.

English language sightseeing tours can be booked from most international hotels. They're called the Hatto Bus and there's a selection of different tours taking either a day or half a day on a large yellow coach with an English-speaking guide. A tour of the town and a boat ride up the Sumida River to Asakusa is a pleasant way to spend an afternoon.

Outside Tokyo – splendid and different

Outside Tokyo the English disappears very quickly. Essentially assume that it's not spoken and plan from there. Kyoto is often on the "places to see" list. During the war it was the only city, along with nearby Nara, that was spared the bombing as it was deemed a city of international cultural interest. However, Japanese construction has pretty much homogenized it since then. Kyoto is a modern, well-developed concrete city, proofed against earthquakes and cabled to provide power and communications to everyone like any other in the world. Japanese people tend to have a very good ability to look through this though, and see the ancient beauty hidden underneath, which is as good a way to appreciate something as any.

Japan is full of natural wonders (when they can be found away from the development of man). A quick search of the Internet will provide a plethora of things to see and places to go. The Shinkansen is fast, efficient and geographically accessible. The local trains make travel simple to even remote locations but it is best to take a map in English as the stations tend to only provide Japanese once away from the metropolitan areas.

Mr, Miss, Mrs, Ms and the meaning of "-san"

If you've ever wondered what the –san means eg in Suzuki-san (and if you haven't experienced this yet, you will) it's a simple honorific title equivalent to Mr, Mrs, Miss or Ms. It actually makes life much easier in written correspondence as you no longer need to be worried about getting it right. One size fits all as it were.

San, being an honorific title, you can reference it to all adults except yourself. Most gaijin faux pas are forgiven with a quizzical look or a polite smile. This one quickly draws irritation as it implies condescension. Therefore, when introducing yourself or, for example, when leaving a message simply use your name. "Smith desu" is the simple format when doing this and is perfectly correct and proper Japanese.

The concept of "oneself" will also extend, in certain circumstances, to colleagues and co-workers in a company. For example, when referring to someone who is your senior to a third party, it is not uncommon to hear the expected "san" be dropped completely. This is not because the speaker is showing any form of disrespect to their colleague, but rather they are showing greater respect to the third party as their colleague could be considered to be an extension of the same "oneself".

It is also common not to offer a first name until you know the person reasonably well, this will most likely make them feel a little uncomfortable until they know you better as it's a little overly friendly but also, as Japanese wouldn't do that, there is a chance that the person will take this to be your surname instead.

You'll notice I mentioned that you can refer to any adult as "-san", that's because children are referred to as –kun for a boy and –chan for a girl. In this instance you'd switch from using the family name to the child's first name when referring to them.

For example, if a young girl's name is Watanabe Aya (Watanabe being the family name), then she'd be referred to as Aya-chan and likewise a boy who's name is Watanabe Ken would be referred to as Ken-kun. This would continue until mid-teens when the first name only might be used, however men and women will continue all their lives to refer to their friends of the same sex by –kun and –chan. It's considered a little familiar to refer to someone of the opposite sex by these prefix and will raise a smile among those around you if you do. If you do, you might just end up with a date that you weren't expecting.

Being exactly wrong rather than inexactly right

One striking feature about Japan is the level of "precision" in all aspects of daily life. I have a theory that, as a result of kanji requiring stroke perfect execution to ensure legibility, one key Japanese characteristic is the desire to always be absolutely "correct". Essentially, a Japanese person would prefer to be exact than approximate. If you ask a foreigner the last time they went skiing they'll tell you last winter. If you ask a Japanese person they'll say January 23rd.

The desire to be precise can lead to significant effort being expended to provide an accurate answer however the concept of what is "accurate" is often overlooked. I have had teams present forecasts to me where they have invested entire weekends to update numbers by less than a fraction of a percent, whilst overlooking the average margin of error for the same forecast was something over ten percent. The result can be summarized that people would prefer to be *exactly wrong rather than inexactly right*.

This may lead to a degree of frustration for a foreigner as an answer is often avoided rather than summarized or alternatively, quoted to an unnecessary degree of precision with an associated unnecessary degree of effort to derive it. Watching the weather report this morning provided a good example of this where the rainfall, following storms overnight, was quoted as being 101.2 millimeters (40.48 inches) of rain. The degree of accuracy is essentially meaningless as there will only be one place where this number is correct and that is in the catchment container. However, approximations are not the norm and "precision" is valued but the cost unrecognized.

Japanese vs Western education – learn to learn

Recently my son had a school project where he had to ask people about how they approached different issues when they were fifteen, for example what was television like or what could a phone do when you were fifteen. One of the interesting questions was how did I approach research when I was that age to which I had to admit it wasn't easy going to a library, finding what looked like the right book from the index cards, actually finding the book and then reading it cover to cover to find the answer. Definitely not as simple as Googling it. When my son asked my wife, who is Japanese, the same question her answer was very different. It had never been a problem for her as she'd never been asked to research anything. The teacher had always just given them the book and told them which pages to learn.

I once arranged for a group of children from my son's school to visit one of my company's flagship stores and meet the staff and ask about how a store works, the role of advertising and how concepts are communicated to consumers. The children had a great day and as I walked them around I asked them questions on different aspects of what they were seeing.

The interesting part for me though came afterwards when the store manager approached me and asked me why I'd been asking the children so many questions. Obviously I'd been making the children think about what they were seeing and to understand by themselves how the store worked and the role of communication in that process. But to me it was an interesting question and I asked the store manager why he'd asked it. He replied that in a Japanese school, the teacher would never have asked a question but would have told the children the answers and would have expected them all to take note and learn. He'd never been encouraged to "figure something out" and had been very surprised to see how the children had responded to it.

This is a good example of the major difference between the Japanese education system and a traditional Western one. More than twenty years ago, one of Japan's senior politicians recognized this and led a cry to change Japan's education system which he saw as a major weakness in the coming world. Little has changed since then and Japan has been in recession for most of the time since his book was published.

He illustrated the point by giving the example of a teacher in a class asking the children a simple question. The first child answers and, if wrong, the teacher says "no" before moving on to the next child. Three in a row are incorrect before one provides the right answer. "Yes", says the teacher and instructs the children to write down the correct answer. He then contrasted this to a Western teacher asking a class of children the same question. The first child answers incorrectly and the teacher responds by saying "no, now explain why you said that".

The Japanese system was designed to impart vast quantities of data to children in a relatively limited time frame. Unfortunately, the system has not changed or adapted to the new world where a single child with an iPhone can take on the might of an entire school of knowledge and win. It is recognized in Japan that something needs to be changed to address this and that it's a potentially major obstacle for the future growth of the economy and country but, discouragingly, little has changed in the past two decades since "A Blue Print for a New Japan" was published calling for a new approach to education.

Start with the detail, then the big picture

A foreigner will typically summarize a situation first, and then move to the detail. Essentially the trunk of the tree is illustrated before the leaves. Japan tends to be the reverse of this and the starting point will be the detail and the summary may be omitted entirely. The automatic assumption from a foreigner will usually be to consider the initial explanation to be the crux of the issue whereas, in reality, it is often the reverse and the actual issue may only emerge after some considerable discussion.

This may lead to confusion initially as the information appears to be flowing in reverse and it becomes necessary to remember all the detail and not only the relevant detail to the situation. Dependent upon the individual, and whether they are prone to longwinded explanations, this can often become problematic.

Explaining the key issue and then adding relevant detail would be considered more efficient. Interestingly, a Japanese person is quite comfortable with the Western approach, it's simply not that natural.

Why is spoken English so difficult?

I was once in a bar in Copenhagen talking to the barman about how English had become the global language by default and he was agreeing with me and adding his opinion on how this would be adopted, not simply as a second language, but fairly quickly as a first language too for the young Internet based generation. And then I realized I was in a bar in Copenhagen talking to a barman in perfect English about English and further I realized that there was no way I could have the counter conversation in Danish, or any other language for that matter, in a bar in England with your average Englishman. *The curse of growing up in a native English speaking country is that it makes mono-linguists of most of us.*

Japan is also, to all intents and purposes, a monolingual society. At a recent government sponsored forum on the internationalization of the country, the Japanese delegation presented in Japanese with translation into English however the Chinese delegation presented in English with translation into Japanese. I have heard many theories as to why this is, from it's a form of government control to the basic sound structure of the language is significantly simpler than English and so pronunciation is more difficult to move from Japanese to English than from English to Japanese. However, having had a bilingual Japanese assistant for many years who's English was often better than my own, I know there is no simple answer to this.

I have European friends who once explained to me that to have a decent, basic conversation in English you need only around 400 words and then you can dive into pretty much any day-to-day discussion. In Japan though, unlike Europe, there is minimal exposure to spoken English and so the chances of picking up these 400 words is very restricted. My European friends would point out that they learnt a lot of their vocabulary fairly young by listening to the radio and English language songs. This doesn't happen in Japan, TV is in Japanese or dubbed (somewhat questionably) into Japanese and only a limited amount of English is actually broadcast. Radio is in a similar situation with Japanese pop dominating the airwaves. So the exposure never happens.

Schooling in English is designed around passing exams and focuses almost exclusively on grammar and vocabulary but not on spoken language or basic communication. *English is incredibly powerful for communication because you can make so many mistakes and still be understood.* Japanese doesn't work that way. In my early days in Japan I asked my manager about this and he explained at length that one of the problems was that when English was reinterpreted in katakana, he would have difficulty working out the real pronunciation and therefore he was hesitant to use it and make a mistake. He was extremely surprised when I asked him what the problem with that was. There are accents in the UK that are incomprehensible even to a native speaker, and so I asked why would he have thought it would worry me if there was a slight mis-pronunciation in the occasional word when talking with Japanese friends. It hadn't occurred to him that errors were fine, and that communication was the important issue.

The end result is that Japan is as monolingual as the UK or most of the USA, it's just monolingual in a language only used in one country rather than in a globally accepted default language. And until the school system is radically changed, it's going to stay that way.

Do I really need a hanko? – and what is it?

That depends. A hanko is a small wooden stamp (sometimes called a "chop" is other parts of Asia) that is used in Japan as a substitute for a signature. As the stamps can be bought from any local stationary store, it's not exactly the most secure method of authorizing documents but it is much more widely accepted in Japan than a conventional signature. In fact, many Japanese people do not actually have a standard signature, which can cause chaos with passport related documents where they're needed overseas.

If you do need a hanko, rather than buying one in a stationary store, you can design it yourself which provides for a nice element of personalization. Any design is allowable, however it is simply more practical to either use your initials or name as you still need to be able to recognize whom it belongs to after it's been used.

As hankos are used for all official documents (bank transfer authorizations, insurance forms, driving applications, in fact, almost anything you can think of) it would seem to be a system particularly open to abuse. Anyone who has possession of a bankbook and the hanko registered to that bankbook can empty the account without having to provide any further form of identification. It's simply taken for granted that if you have the hanko in your hand, you are the owner of the contents of that account. This can, and very much does, lead to problems and especially older people tend to be victims of a relative deciding it's time to empty the bank account. However, it is the accepted approach and the way the entire economy operates.

In general, as a foreigner, you can live in Japan without a hanko. This is probably the best approach when you are unused to the power they wield and if you do decide to have one, avoid using it for authorizing your bank account. However, there are times when this becomes a necessity, for example if you are buying property, without a hanko it simply isn't going to happen. In this instance you will need a *registered* hanko, whereby you have taken it to the local ward office and completed the documentation to register your hanko to yourself. You become the owner of that specific hanko, hence a personalized design is a good idea. At this point, whatever you do, do not lose that stamp. It is officially you and can authorize almost anything in your name as it is considered proof of your identity, no matter who is actually using it.

The obvious question then is why not use a signature in place of a hanko, after all, it's more convenient, your signature is always with you, it's significantly harder to forge and it's the ultimate in personalization. The answer is simply one of trust. Japanese people are used to hankos and have little experience of using a signature. People don't trust them and are convinced they are simple to forge, though every one of my friends who has ever mentioned this has been unable to copy my signature in anything close to a form resembling the original. The upshot it that hankos are here to stay, avoid them if you can but you need to accept you'll be in a very small minority if you believe they're a problem.

Who really rules the roost?

It would be fair to say men still tend to have better career prospects in Japan than women. The number of women on executive boards of listed companies can probably be counted on one hand. Even at a non-executive level, women tend to be excluded from the promotion ladder. As was once stated by one of the few highly successful women in corporate Japan, "there isn't actually a glass ceiling, just a thick layer of men".

Within domestic companies there remains a tacit understanding that the preferential roles are the preserve of men. Women, irrespective of education, seniority or career path, will leave a company once they become married.

However, for the regular salaryman, this becomes a more complex picture. The household purse strings are firmly held by the wife. She will provide a weekly allowance to her husband and he must survive on it for both his lunches at work and any social activities in the evening. Whereas women accept that they are expected to leave a company when married, men accept that they will surrender their monthly paycheck to their wives.

Honne and Tatemae – the face and the feeling

The concept of honne, *your true thoughts and beliefs* and tatemae, *your public face*, is key in Japanese culture. At all times face must be maintained and honor served as it were. This comes at the cost of the true feelings and beliefs of the individual though.

In Western culture there is the familiar concept of a white lie, an untruth that is used to make the truth more palatable such as saying "nice to see you again" where in reality you sincerely wish you hadn't seen them again. It's polite, costs nothing and the facade of geniality is maintained.

Honne and tatemae however, can go significantly deeper than a simple white lie. The surface position will be maintained at all costs and the truth, once covered over, will become almost impossible to uncover.

If ever you are in a discussion and you have the feeling that there is something else going on but you are unsure what it actually is, this is what you are experiencing. Somewhere there is a position being maintained but it is extremely difficult to identify what it is without help.

This is where your Japanese bridge comes in. In your early days in Japan it is very helpful to develop a close relationship with someone you trust, who can act as your bridge between Japanese and Western culture. When you believe there is a sub-plot you are not aware of, this is the person to turn to who will be able to explain to you what it is that you are not understanding.

In some instances, the position taken to cover a truth may actually appear juvenile or ridiculous to someone new to Japan. However, the important aspect of this is to recognize that there is a secondary issue in the first place, only then can you begin to try to address it. The position being presented is merely a subtext to the actual issue.

For example, when someone resigns from a company it is reasonably common for them to say it is for "family reasons", they have a sick mother or their father wants them to join the family firm. Although these reasons may be true, it's telling that I've never had someone resign because they didn't like their manager, were bored of what they were doing or had simply found a better job. The truth, honne, may be one of these issues but the face, tatemae, will always be simply "family reasons".

Sempai – Kohai, the teacher and the taught

You will often hear people refer to someone as their *sempai* although there may be no obvious relationship between the two. Sempai approximates to "senior" in the sense of a teacher/pupil style of reference and *kohai* refers to the "junior". The relationships are often established at a young age, for example, if two people went to the same university but one was in the senior year when the other joined, they would forever be the sempai and the younger would forever be recognized as the kohai.

The reference to this relationship is usually only referred to directly by the kohai, it would be highly unusual for the sempai to actually state that they are the sempai, this being seen as somewhat unnecessary and in slightly poor taste.

The relationship remains important throughout a person's life, the sempai is expected to provide support and advice and the kohai is expected to show due respect, almost deference, to the other. This has some difficult or awkward consequences when the two work closely together. If the kohai is promoted above the sempai, the relationship remains unchanged and the expectations are still in place. It can in fact become quite difficult in a working environment if this occurs. However, the relationship is important to both parties and provides a sense of unity. It may seem odd that a happening of circumstance would lead to a lifelong association where one individual is seen as the senior of the other but it will always remain important to the individuals themselves.

1966 – where did all the babies go?

A Japanese friend of mine recounted once that at school they had been in a very large class of over forty children, however, in the year above them, each class had less than thirty children. The decline in the birth rate from 1965 to 1966 was, in fact, something akin to the decline during the Second World War. This is because 1966 was the year of *hinoeuma*, a year when superstition holds that a baby girl born in this year would be bad luck for life. And not being able to decide whether a baby would be a boy or a girl, the entire nation simply tried not to have children that year. The year only occurs every sixty years so it can be expected that this will repeat itself in 2026 as people remain inclined to some certain superstitions. The class of 2044 will be a lot emptier than the class of 2045.

Can Japanese people drink? – bears / woods?

Oh yes. However, people tend to fall into two groups, those that can drink in a way that would be considered normal in Western countries, and those who turn bright red at the first drop of alcohol and often then proceed to quickly fall asleep. People in this group tend to refer to themselves as "weak drinkers" and will often avoid alcohol entirely of an evening or limit to a single glass of wine stretched over the course of a dinner.

I've been invited to dinner on more than one occasion where my host would start a lively conversation, have a few drinks and then quietly fall asleep at the table leaving the remaining guests to enjoy the dinner. Interestingly, this rarely seems to lead to awkward situations and the conversation tends to continue around them until they wake up naturally later.

There is actually a reason for this alcohol intolerance in that Japanese, and to an extent, people of Asian descent in general, lack an enzyme that processes alcohol in the body. In some ways this is a good thing as it reduces the overall alcohol intake however it does mean missing out on many an interesting evening.

The upshot of this alcohol intolerance is that, if you see a drunk salaryman staggering along the road towards the train station, you can never actually be sure whether they have had a glass of wine or the entire bottle. As a result, *there tends to be less of a stigma attached to becoming intoxicated in a public* setting and people are generally forgiving of those who imbibe too much of an evening.

A couple of stories of kindness

It has to be said that I've been lucky over the years and have always appreciated the kindness shown to me. When I first moved into an apartment in Osaka just weeks after landing in Japan, my phone was still to be connected. These were the days before mobile phones and the Internet and I'd been out of contact with my friends and family for several weeks by this time. I arranged for the phone to be installed and on the day hurried home to make my first contact since I'd arrived in Japan.

I was really not happy when, after all the pain to arrange everything, the actual phone itself didn't work. I called the building manager, a wonderful lady in her mid-thirties who spoke not a word of English. I managed to show her the problem and although we couldn't communicate she smiled and went away. I still remember that feeling of loneliness with all my hopes of speaking to home disappearing.

Ten minutes later there was a knock on the door and there she was with her five-year old daughter with a big smile on her face holding their own phone for me to plug in and use. I've never forgotten that kindness and understanding or the little girl with the smile, now probably a grown woman with children of her own.

Another early example occurred soon after I arrived in Japan to live in Osaka and I was invited to a night out in a nearby city of Kobe. The evening went on late and inevitably I ended up missing the last train back. My friends kindly put me up and in the morning I started the journey home only to realize I had no idea at all where I was or how to find the station.

At least I knew its name and so asked a lady on her bicycle where it was, using sign language and continuous repetition. She probably thought I was from another planet but she still stepped off her bicycle and to my surprise started to walk with me. I'd expected her to simply point but she continued to walk with me for fifteen minutes or more and eventually led me to the station entrance. Then, still without a word, she got back on her bicycle and rode off the way we'd come. I'll never forget the kindness either or the little wave she gave as she rode away. The Japanese people, as a whole, can be incredibly generous of spirit.

Karaoke – the great stress buster

Karaoke is famously a national passion in Japan. And it's totally different from anything experienced elsewhere. Whereas in Western countries, a karaoke song is usually performed in open bars by a semi-inebriated businessman who is generally entertaining the audience at the price of his dignity, in Japan, everyone is with you and it is a great night out. It's also really good for releasing stress after a long hard day and if Japan is getting to you, treat yourself to a night and you'll feel much better.

Whether you're amazing or just plain rubbish, your crowd enjoys the extent of how hard you are trying rather than how you perform. The more effort you put into it, the greater the appreciation of those around you. You should remember though that *there are only two times when the crowd goes quiet, when the singer is amazing and when the singer is utter rubbish*. If you find yourself with a microphone and a silent crowd, you should assess the situation.

Typically in Japan, karaoke is a group event. Friends or work colleagues will go together and hire a box. You book the box by time (two hours is a good starting point) but you will be required to leave when your time is up so if you think you're out for a big night, book for longer as you're unlikely to be able to extend your time on a busy night.

You order drinks and snacks via the telephone on the wall (there will be one) but the staff are very unlikely to speak English so speak slowly and repeat your order several times and hang up. With a bit of luck they'll get the idea.

If it's your first time at karaoke, unless you are a very talented singer, don't try Queen or Simon and Garfunkel. You're more than likely to crash and burn! And always remember *the golden rule of karaoke, sing the songs you know, not the ones you like.*

Not all karaoke bars have English language songs but if you stick to the big chains, like Big Echo, you should be OK. You can rent a karaoke box from a small one for four people up to large rooms that can host a party. The key is to enjoy yourself and join in the spirit of the evening. There is nothing funnier than watching your friend up on stage leading the crowd in the motions to YMCA with a happy waitress in a fireman's lift over his shoulder. Join in and enjoy.

Another useful aspect of karaoke is keeping the kids entertained on a Saturday afternoon. Rent two karaoke boxes, put the kids in one, enter twenty tunes into the system and retire next door to the other box. The kids will love it and you will be able to enjoy an hour's peace and quiet.

Bars, clubs and a hundred dollars for a beer

Stories of being ripped off in a bar and having to pay hundreds (if not thousands of dollars) are sadly true and relatively common but partly arise from misunderstanding and false expectations rather than something distinctly untoward.

Many bars will have a cover charge. This is a fixed fee per person simply to sit at a table (and sometimes be served with a small dish or snack). A cover charge should usually be around ¥1,000 per person, more than this and you're in an expensive location. There's no negotiation about this. If you want to be in the bar, you're going to have to pay the cover charge if they have one.

Especially in Tokyo, don't expect prices to be the same as at home. You're in the largest metropolis on the planet, the price is going to be different. However a little preparation should remove the main shocks for you.

Japan is famous for its hostess bars where young women are paid to laugh at your jokes, fill up your beer and generally make you feel welcome and relaxed. If you think about it though, this is not dissimilar to what a barmaid in Europe or America is paid to do. A hostess bar does not come with additional "services" supplied, it's simply a bar, though in some cases it can be a very expensive bar. However, be aware that if a girl sits at your table, you will be paying for her time even if you didn't ask her to join you.

Mostly, unless you are actually taken by a Japanese colleague, you won't find yourself in the seriously expensive locations, you simply won't see them, or the gentleman on the door will let you know they're full and maybe you should look elsewhere. If you don't speak Japanese and don't know what you're getting yourself into, don't be put out by this advice, he's saving you potentially thousands of dollars and, as only Japanese will be spoken, a potentially dull evening as well.

If you are on your own or in a group that's unused to Japan, when you enter a bar it's fine to ask if there's a cover charge and in fact, in most instances, they'll ask you if it's OK and once you order your first drink you'll have a good idea of the potential cost of the place and how your evening will work out.

Although this is not a guidebook, at this point I have to mention an area around Shibuya station that, if you get the chance before it's demolished, is worth a visit by everyone. Post-war the Japanese government wanted to create areas where the average person could go to relax in an evening and so they created an entire industry of areas where small bars would grow up next to each other. By small I mean four people can sit in there and then it's full. Over the years most of these have disappeared and now only two districts remain, one in Shinkjuku and one in Shibuya.

Come out of Shibuya station at Hachiko Crossing and walk clockwise until you're under the railway tracks. Cross the road and walk up the small side road with the tracks on your left. After about 50m you'll see a little alleyway on your right. Walk into it and suddenly you're in a different land. There are 47 bars each the size of a small dining table and can take four or five people at a time and then are full. They're an amazing site to see and an experience to indulge in. The owners are always friendly, as are the patrons who will often insist on you joining even when you're a group of four and there's only one chair free. Everyone will squash up and you'll have instant friends for the evening. If you get the chance also take a look upstairs at the "function room". The stairs will be near vertical and the room no larger than the refrigerator in the corner. A wonderful place to spend an evening and I'm always impressed when the mama-san makes her way up the stair case, drinks tray in hand, just to check that everything is alright. As I say, if you get the chance, visit these bars before they're gone, they're a wonderful piece of Japanese history and tradition.

Hachiko – a dog's life

The story of Hachiko is famous in Japan and to some extent around the world following the success of the movie "Shall We Dance" in which it features quite highly. Hachiko was a little Akita dog in the 1930s, intensely loyal to his master. Everyday he would walk with him to Shibuya station and then wait patiently until his master came home in the evening. One day his master passed away at the office. Hachiko waited for him to return and never left his spot, eventually, after several days, dying from hunger and thirst. People were so moved by this that they donated funds for a statue of Hachiko to be erected outside the station where it still stands today and has become the most popular meeting place in Tokyo.

It always struck me though, the funds would probably have been better used to feed the poor dog in the first place, but then again, where would people meet if that had been the case.

Matsuri, yukata and a portable shrines

You can always tell when a summer festival is going to take place as you'll see strings of lanterns being strung up over the preceding few days. Listen out on the day and you'll probably be able to hear when everything starts and then simply go along and join in the fun.

Japan loves a good festival. They seem to occur pretty much all year around whether they're the New Year Festivals, spring, summer, hanami or for any other reason, you'll see the lanterns go up and people change into yukata (light summer gowns) and the beers come out, but the summer ones are the most followed, in large part as the weather is usually the best at this time of year for a party.

The festivals are always good fun and usually represent an entire neighborhood coming together for one reason or another. The pleasure comes in it being a social event for everyone whether they're young children or great grand parents. They often involve a stylized form of dance centered around a raised stage where the drummer will sit striking the beat for everyone to dance to.

If you experience a matsuri, you'll be welcomed in by everyone there to either join in or simply stand at the side and watch the activities develop through an evening. If you think you have the hang of the dance feel free to join in, everyone will be very welcoming. Often, an evening festival will be preceded by a procession through the center of a neighborhood carrying what looks like a miniature shrine. Children will join in with the singing as the men of the neighborhood carry the shrine (omikoshi) on their shoulders, chanting and singing as they go.

If you see this, it's fine to join the followers behind the shrine but typically, those actually carrying it are an organized group and it's best to let them continue without trying to join in directly. And if you follow the shrine to the end of the procession you're bound to find the starts of the evening events and the beer.

Although most are small, local affairs, some of the events are extremely well organized and on a citywide basis. I once attended a summer festival in the city of Kobe only to see omikoshi three stories high with men clinging to the top as they were raced through the streets and round buildings. One crash would bring the entire edifice tumbling down. And then everyone would laugh, climb back onto the shrine and carry on again.

Adulthood; all on the same day

Twenty is an important marker on the road to adulthood in Japan. Although legally it has minimal implications, similar to turning twenty one in Western countries, it's a recognition that you are no longer a child.

The celebration of becoming twenty is effectively recognized twice; once on the actual birthday when people may now legally drink and secondly on the second Monday of January, when the country celebrates together the coming of age of anyone who's twentieth birthday was in the previous year. It's so important in the Japanese calendar it's actually been established as a national holiday since 1948.

This is actually one of my favorite days of the year as you will see hundreds of young women, walking around town in the most breathtaking kimono (technically, with long sleeves it's called a furisode). Go down to the main social meeting areas in whichever city you are in at around lunch time and you will see a truly "only in Japan" moment. And remember to take a camera with you!

Omiage – the little gifts to bring back home

If you pass through a Japanese airport and wonder why there are so many stores selling little snacks or souvenirs, it's due to the tradition of always bringing back a little gift for friends or work colleagues from the trip you're returning from. The gift is called *omiage* pronounced o-me-a-ge.

Omiage becomes a large part of travelling and an important element of social politeness. It's almost expected that, whether on vacation or on business, you would remember those back home and bring them something from your travels. This becomes quite an obligation if you travel regularly on business. In this case you essentially have three options.

The first one is to comply with the tradition and always bring something back. This is good Japanese think, but quickly becomes quite onerous. The second is to completely ignore tradition and pretend that, being a foreigner, you know nothing about it. The third is to be targeted. If you have an assistant or secretary, these are the people who would appreciate it most and the relationship is close enough to explain that you won't always bring something for them but you do always appreciate them. Essentially you will be gaining points for the effort and recognition of Japanese etiquette and it will only cost you the occasional box of chocolates.

The concept of giri – the unspoken obligation

Japan is nothing if not based around the concept of the unspoken obligation. It is very similar to the Western idea of owing someone a favor, however, in this case it differs from the point that it is a favor to be returned without asking and would never be called in.

In the office environment, when a man receives chocolates on Valentine's day, they are most likely to be *giri*, given under a recognized obligation such as the female secretary to her male boss. It doesn't mean she likes him but rather that she is recognizing a social expectation. And as a result, the boss is then under the same obligation to return a gift on White Day in March.

Omiage, the souvenir from your travels is also giri, an expectation from receiver and sense of obligation from the giver of a small token gift from your vacation.

Giri is significantly more that just the concept of a favor though and manifests as a real sense of social obligation. Not returning a favor is one thing and reflects poorly in the eyes of the one to whom it was owed. Not recognizing giri is a act looked down on by the entire society.

Interestingly, the Japanese word for mother-in-law is *giri no haha* which directly translates as "obligation mother".

Pachinko – the opiate of the masses

Stepping off the main streets and into the darker alleys of most cities in Japan, you will find the ubiquitous Pachinko parlor. Pachinko is a addictive game and you will probably hear it before you see it, rows and rows of what look like slot machines with ball bearings streaming down them from above making a deafening cacophony of sound. The player, usually almost trance like, turns a small handle marginally left or right to guide the balls into the winning slots at the bottom. Pachinko is a solitary game, people rarely even talk to each other, however it brings a hypnotic state of relief and remains immensely popular despite the rise of modern gaming and alternative pastimes.

Although gambling is severely restricted in Japan, Pachinko is in essence a simple form of gambling despite this. The player purchases the metal balls for cash and then plays the game. If lucky, a player will then win spoons or tokens as they continue to feed cash into the game. When they've finished they may have won a basketful of spoons for their days efforts. These, not being cash, ensures that pachinko remains within the law. There will also, usefully, be a small store somewhere near the entrance that buys spoons and sells them back to the Pachinko Parlor. The player has the cash, the Parlor has everyone else's cash plus the spoons, and everybody is happy.

Pachinko, predominantly run by North Koreans and a major source of currency for the Pyongyang regime, is so addictive it also leads to tragedy each summer as mothers leave young children strapped into cars with the air conditioning running whilst they go inside to play their favorite pastime. Only too regularly are there reports of the car running out of gasoline and the temperature rises to the point the child cannot survive. Each and every summer.

Politics – what happened to democracy?

Japan, in theory, is a multi-party democracy and in the last five years it has actually proved that control can move from one party to another and back again, something that hadn't effectively occurred since the creation of the modern constitutional democracy after the war.

In reality, the role of the opposition is taken internally within the ruling party and the public opposition is little more than a distraction. Within the LDP, the current ruling party, there are multiple different factions each with a faction leader and each with a loyal following of diet members.

Constituencies are often held within a family and it is common to see a seat being transferred through multiple generations of one particular family. The loyalties to the faction then can be old and run deep.

It is these factions, underneath the veil of a single party, that create the opposition to each other. Policies are discussed and largess decided behind closed doors because the opposition is, effectively, in-house and therefore not questioned in public.

As a result, the position of Prime Minister becomes almost ceremonial with few having both party and public support. It therefore also becomes a continuously revolving door which can be seen in that, as of writing, there have been ten premierships and nine prime ministers (Shinzo Abe having held office twice) in Japan since the year 2000. And, added to this, you have to remember that Koizumi was there for six of those years.

Effectively the Prime Minister becomes a compromise candidate of the various factions and, rather than attempt to influence government through debate, the Prime Minister may be simply changed if it becomes more expedient in exacting legislation. Given the necessities and obligations to address all aspects of society, it could arguably be considered operational communism. Politics simply works in a different way in Japan than it does in a Western democracy.

Whales – do they really taste that good?

Each year Japan harvests some four hundred or more minke whales for scientific purposes. In an unrecognized twist of irony, the scientific research is actually to monitor the aging of the whale population (you count the layers of earwax like tree rings, not easy if the whale is still alive). Somehow the whale meat then finds its way to tables of diners across Japan.

Whaling is big business in Japan and the industry has cleverly side stepped the ethical issues around eating whale meat by appealing to Japan's sense of historic culture by saying Japanese people have always eaten whale and it's a tradition that's part of the national character. True, but only just. Pre-war, Japan ate no more whale meat that the English, French or Americans. It was only during the 1950s and '60s that a significant increase in whale consumption occurred as the country looked for a cheap food supply to support a growing population. In reality Japan has no ancient tradition of eating whales; but don't try telling anyone that, the industry has done their job well at convincing people otherwise.

I once asked my assistant what she would tell her grandchildren when all the whales were gone. She looked at me and thought seriously about this for a while before saying "they were tasty". At least she was honest to herself.

There is some discussion of converting whaling boats and ports to support a more tourist friendly approach and to develop a whale watching industry instead of a whale consuming one however this is very much an idea in development and has yet to catch the national psyche in a way that will drive genuine change. In reality though, whale meat is not on the menu of every restaurant in Japan and unless you specifically go looking, you're very unlikely to actually find it.

Why do teacups come in sets of five?

Although at first sight, when visiting the home of a Japanese friend, it may appear that they have lost a cup from a set of six, you'll soon notice that the plates are also in sets of five, the knives and forks are sets of five and in fact everything in the house that comes in a set will have come in a set of an odd number.

This is an interesting example of where Western nature is to automatically feel comfortable with even numbers, Japan is more comfortable with odd numbers. This can be seen everywhere from wedding gifts where the money is always an odd number to the failure of the two thousand yen note to become popular largely as it represented an even rather than odd number.

The actual answer is not that they have lost a cup or a plate but that sets in a house will always be in odd numbers as it is seen as a symbol of good fortune that it can't be easily divided. The home will always stay together and remains a place of safety and refuge.

Wedding gifts – a really nice envelope

Japanese weddings are expensive. Very expensive. The average cost in Nagoya, the city reputedly where the most is lavished on the happy couple, is over ¥5 million, or $50,000. As a result, it's traditional to give money as a gift at a wedding rather than any form of present. In fact, if you do want to give a traditional Western style gift, do this in the days after the wedding and not actually at the time as no one will understand what you're doing.

The value of your gift will depend on your relation to the happy couple. If you are friends, ¥10,000 (~$100) or ¥30,000 would be appropriate. If you are the boss, then ¥50,000 would be closer to the mark. Notice however, that, as discussed elsewhere, the amount you give should never be an even number. This would be extremely bad luck as it's suggesting the couple may need to divide the money later if they get divorced.

The other point to be aware of is that the actual notes should always be pristine and provided in an intricate white envelope used especially for weddings (be careful when buying this from your local convenience store, the ones for funerals look remarkably similar and would not go down well on the day). Banks will actually provide notes especially for wedding gifts but in the absence of this it's important that the notes you use are not creased or show any signs of use. It's a gift after all. On your way into the wedding you'll see a tray near the door where the envelopes are presented. Ensure your name is inside so they know who it's from or including a little card with a short message is a simple solution for foreigners without great skills in kanji.

I once saw a foreigner provide the notes in a brown, regular envelope and, not knowing to leave it at the door, walked up to the bride and groom and presented it directly to them, pulling it, somewhat crumpled, from his pocket. That was over ten years ago and people still talk about it today. Money may not be a standard Western style gift but there is still a nice etiquette about it and you're helping the young couple defray a significant cost incurred on the day.

Nailing Santa to the Cross

Japan isn't a Christian country (though there is a small Christian population) and Christmas isn't a national holiday, simply a normal working day. However, there is much around Christmas that is enjoyed and some "Japan only" traditions too. In the 1990s Kentucky Fried Chicken ran a Christmas commercial with the tag line "Christmas isn't Christmas without Kentucky Fried Chicken". The campaign was a huge hit and still to this day you'll see queues of people outside your local KFC's, booking ticket in hand, collecting their buckets of chicken wings to enjoy the next day.

Christmas Eve is also the day for a hot date. If you are single then on Christmas Eve you must be seen to have a date or you'll generally be considered a complete loser. I've even seen ladies in the office dressing up, declaring they have a date to everyone (something very unusual in Japan) and then bumped into them later in a bar or a restaurant where they've met up with another girlfriend who also didn't have a date but didn't want the world to know.

There is often confusion as well around how to celebrate Christmas. Plastic trees are now quite common (though cripplingly expensive) and the lights and decorations start to appear as early as

October. It is also a busy shopping period with the busiest day of the year usually falling on the 23rd December which is the Emperor Akihito's birthday and accordingly a national holiday. So people do get into the spirit of Christmas in as much as gifts are presented and the stores play carols.

Sometimes things don't quite go right. There is a wonderful story, that may most likely be an urban myth (but having lived here for a while you can see how it is possibly true) of a department store in Ginza having an intricate Christmas display. The lights were shining, the tree was as big as could fit in the store and the central display was a life-size cross with Santa firmly nailed to it. At least they tried.

Celebrating Easter and Thanksgiving

Doesn't happen. Neither Easter nor Thanksgiving are celebrated in Japan in any material sense. Both being Christian festivals, and Japan not being a Christian country, there is little recognition. Indeed, I have been asked many times over the years if we even celebrate Thanksgiving in the UK. Thanksgiving being a specific US event, the actual answer is obviously no. However, an English friend of mine has a better answer, when asked the question he replies "yes, but we celebrate it in March when they left".

If you do celebrate Easter and Thanksgiving, the big international department stores will be able to provide Easter Eggs and turkey so it is possible to plan family events if this is something you would like to do. You will need to book a turkey in advance as the concept of an eight-kilogram (seventeen-pound) turkey is not well recognized in the market and the limited supply can sometimes be by order only.

Trick or Treat – though mostly treat

Strangely, given the lack of recognition of Christian events, Halloween has become quite widely celebrated across Japan. Children will dress up and "Trick or Treat" parades will be organized locally all across the country. People make quite an effort and the kids really enjoy themselves though if you ask, few will actually understand the origins of Halloween itself, it's just seen as a great day out for the family to enjoy.

You will be welcomed to join your local event though in some cases you may be asked to make a contribution to the organization although this would normally be ¥1~2,000. There will also be a map to follow showing which houses are involved as it's not quite a random event where any door is fair game. Following the local residents is the simplest approach however, although the concept of the "treat" is well established, the idea of a "trick" is not, hence the need for the map to guide you to the house where the treat awaits.

Valentine's and White Day – Remarkable!

Valentine's Day is an important day on the national calendar however obviously with a Japan twist to it. On Valentine's Day the girl has to give the boy of her affections a gift. Note, only the girl has to give a gift, the boy has another month to plan for it. Chocolate makers and marketers have successfully waged a campaign to persuade the country that Valentine's Day is for girls to provide a gift and that March 14th, White Day, is the day for the boy to respond. For the boy this is wonderful as he knows who he needs to give a gift in return, no embarrassing unrequited affection, however for the girl, she still has the age-old problem of "does he, doesn't he?"

In the office environment, Valentine's and White Day are also recognized but more in the context of the Japanese *giri* or obligation. A secretary has to provide chocolates to her boss. If you receive chocolates from your secretary, don't panic, she is not telling you she hold a secret flame for you, she is simply following recognized custom. You may actually receive several sets of chocolate and always be sure to make a note of who they are from. This is so that on White Day in March you can return the favor and provide flowers or chocolates to all the ladies who recognized you on Valentine's Day. It's generally considered very bad form not to return the gift so make sure you keep the list somewhere safe!

The food – some of the best in the world

Japan has some of the best food in the world and the best restaurants to go with it. Currently, Tokyo boasts more Michelin stars than Paris and wherever you go you will find first-rate service whether it be the most expensive or the most cost friendly establishment in town.

Japanese food boasts a huge variety of both ingredients and styles. Here are a few of the more common:

Sushi (thin sliced raw fish on rice) tastes nothing like you'd expect if you've never tried it before. The overwhelming sense is one of melting texture as you take your first bite. It simply melts in your mouth, no chewing, nothing slimy, just a wonderful experience. Sushi can come in many different forms from tuna slices to fish roe or even sea urchin. Some are more of an acquired taste than others but if you've never tried sushi before, you are missing out.

Sashimi (thin slices raw fish without rice). The difference between sushi and sashimi is simply that sushi comes with rice and sashimi is without rice. Overall sashimi is considered to be the higher in quality but in effect, unless you really know your sushi and sashimi, you really won't notice a difference. Sashimi, being eaten on its own and gently dipped in soy sauce, tends to be limited to fish meat rather than such things as fish roe but that doesn't mean it can't be.

Yaki... yaki simply means cooked and so you'll see it use in conjunction with many different types of food:

Yakiniku (cooked meat). Yakiniku is served as a place of raw meat that you cook yourself over an open fire in the middle of the table. This allows you to cook it to your own taste and everyone around the table can have something different. The types of meat offered are usually varieties of beef, pork or seafood. Tongue is also a favorite for yakiniku, though also something of an acquired taste.

Yakitori (cooked chicken). Yakitori will usually come as pieces of chicken cooked on a wooden skewer, however it may also be served as chicken wings or chicken cartilage so be sure what you're ordering if you don't want a surprise.

Ishiyaki (meat cooked on a hot stone). Ishiyaki is not too common but is an interesting variant on yakiniku and fun to try. It is actually a style of cooking rather than a type of food but is predominantly used for cooking meat though other foods may also be an option or speciality of a particular restaurant.

Sumiyaki (again a style of cooking with food cooked over hot charcoal). Almost anything can be cooked over charcoal from mushrooms to steak. Typically you will order a fixed set menu and so everyone will have the same food throughout the course, all cooking at the same time. Kobe beef cooked in this way is a particular delicacy as it simply melts when you bite into it.

Shabu shabu (cooking in a pan of boiling water). The name shabu shabu comes from the Japanese word for the motion of cooking your food by stirring it backwards and forwards in the water. It will usually come with at least two bowls of different sauces (one soy based and one sesame based) to add flavor to meat or vegetable. It's important here to always remember to dip your food into one of the sauces as this not only adds flavor but also cools the food as well. Remember, you've just cooked it in boiling water. It is going to be hot, do not try eating it directly or you're going to burn yourself here. Here I must provide a nod of thanks to an old friend who actually demonstrated this to me on one of his early visits to Japan. And he still remembers the experience well.

Kaiseki (various small assorted dishes). Kaiseki dishes are small and many. The content will vary from restaurant to restaurant with the general theme of having a little taste of a lot of different dishes. If you want variety, this is the option to try.

Izakaya. An Izakaya is actually a place to eat rather than a type or style of food itself however it will have the common theme of everything being very low priced and also almost always served with beer. If you're looking for a "value" night out, an Izakaya is the place to go.

Catch me if you can – said the shrimp

I've been lucky enough over the years to have travelled the world fairly broadly. I've had chance to eat at some of the finest restaurants there are but am just as happy sitting in a corner table eating noodles from a bowl. But I have never experienced the breadth of variety and quality of food as I have in Japan. It is spectacular though depending on your home country, you may need to suspend your pre-conceptions for a while.

Odori-ebi: otherwise known as "Dancing Shrimp". Live shrimp are dropped into a glass bowl of sake and slowly swim round becoming more and more intoxicated. Eventually the chef will fish one out for you and simply break its back open presenting you with the live flesh to bite directly into. The shrimp is well past caring at this point though you do feel it as it goes down.

Live fish soup: this is presented to you as a small bowl of soup that you drink directly holding the bowl up to your mouth and using a deep spoon to drink the contents. The soup is dark brown and it's only as you are about to take the first mouthful that you realize it's teeming with tiny little fish all swimming frantically around. Don't chew! Close your eyes and swallow as quickly as you can the first time. You do feel these going down too and it's best not to think about what they're doing inside of you. I lived to tell the tale though.

Fugu: this is the famous blowfish and highly toxic. Chefs must be specially licensed to serve fugu and still each year a handful of people will die trying to prepare this at home. It's generally eaten by thrill seekers though it's not much of a thrill as deaths in a licensed restaurant are about as common as meteor strikes. You'll have no problem at all though if you are still concerned, you will have about forty minutes between the onset of the first symptoms of fugu poisoning (lips becoming numb and turning blue) and actual death. You just need to know you're within distance of a local hospital and you'll be fine. The only issue I have about eating fugu is that it's actually one of the blandest forms of sashimi there is. There are so many different forms of wonderful tasting fish that I actually find it a bit of a let down to have this particular one. The best form of fugu though is fuguhire-zake which is a warmed sake with baked fugu fins added for flavor. It's usually ignited in front of you and after the flames are out, it's a delicious new flavor of sake to try.

Basashi: otherwise known as horse sashimi. Basashi is a delicacy of Kyushu, the southern main island in Japan. Horse is widely eaten around the world though in some countries (UK being a good example) people would probably react with horror at the concept of eating horse flesh. However, basashi, served as thinly sliced raw meat, is delicious. It's not that common to find it in Tokyo but a little research and you will find restaurants that specialize in this particular delicacy.

Takoyaki: a late night favorite after a few too many beers have been sampled. Takoyaki is cooked balls of dough with diced chunks of octopus inside. Think of a dumpling with octopus in the center. You will see stalls at the side of roads serving this all across Japan and it is delicious, usually coming in a small plastic container and covered is thick brown sauce and mayonnaise. Eaten using a tooth pick or chopsticks, make sure you test the temperature first. Very fresh and it'll burn your mouth. Let it cool a little and then enjoy. The kids love it too.

Natto: natto is fermented soybean, eaten as a slimy mush that smells like baby sick. You may be able to guess from this description it's actually one of the very few foods in Japan I just can't face. I've tried it but that's enough, time for me to keep clear. However, Japanese people, especially expectant mothers swear by its health giving properties; I guess there must be something going for it as taste, smell and texture are definitely not on the positives list for this particular delicacy.

Anko: Red Bean Buns, watch out for these. The bun will look like a regular doughnut and if you're in the mood, actually looks very appealing. However when you bite into it you'll find the center has been filled with a thick red bean paste. It actually tastes quite nice but once you've bitten into it, you'll be chewing for a long time.

Interestingly, in Japan people don't generally eat rabbit as they're considered pets and too cute to consume. I usually point out to my Japanese friends that they also make excellent gloves but on the whole this doesn't assist in persuading them to try it. Another interesting example is that it wasn't until a Japanese friend pointed it out but lamb is not too common either, being considered to have too strong an odor that lodges itself into clothing.

Beer without food – almost unthinkable

Japanese people enjoy a drink as much as anyone else. It is very common for people to socialize after work and catch up with friends in the evening. The bars of Shibuya to Shinsaibashi are never empty of an evening and to some extent, for the average salaryman, it is almost expected they will spend an evening in the company of their colleagues.

However, Japanese people enjoy eating while they drink too, even if just a snack. It is extremely uncommon for people simply to go for a drink as would be common in a Western bar or pub. If you are ever asked by a Japanese colleague if you would like to go "for a drink" ensure you don't eat before hand. There will be food there and potentially an entire dinner waiting for you.

Sake – what, and what not, to drink

Sake (pronounced *sah-keh*, not *sa-ki*) is both the word for the drink we're familiar with but also the general word for alcohol. You may find it being referred to as *nihon-shu,* which is a little like calling it the "national drink" in concept. Whatever you call it, sake is an entire world unto itself.

Although often referred to in the West as rice wine, the process to make sake is actually closer to brewing beer, but given its usual 14% alcohol it also tends to be served more akin to wine.

As with wines there are limitless varieties of sake, different qualities, different preparations, vintages, sources of water and so on. The flavor depends on many things including how cold the winter was as this affects the rice, how polished the rice is that's being used (the more polished, the higher the quality as a rule of thumb), however, you probably just want to have a drink of sake and enjoy an evening.

The main distinction between sakes, similar to red or white wine is whether you'd like a hot or a cold, sake. Although Hollywood has brought everyone up thinking sake is only drunk hot, in reality, the hot sakes tend to be the lower quality ones where they are being heated to drive off excess cooking alcohol that's been added to fortify the taste. On the whole, try hot sake for the experience, but don't try too much or you'll still be experiencing it the next day. Hot sake, or *atsukan*, is also popular on a cold winters evening and will drive away the chill, at least for a while.

Cold sake, or *reishu*, is generally considered the higher quality or the two types of sake, as it can be served directly and can carry a very refined taste.

The next differentiation is whether you would prefer a dry, (*karakuchi*), or sweet (*amakuchi*), sake. This is entirely down to your personal preference and the quality is no longer the question. To help you, you'll see that there is usually a numbering system in the menu. The higher the number (positive or negative) the drier or sweeter the sake is. This gives you a good reference point through an evening as you try different flavors and styles.

Sake is generally consumed without ice or water, simply enjoy it directly from the bottle and chill it, if you have the opportunity, to improve the experience. Many times in restaurants you'll see people drinking something that looks like sake but they are mixing it with water or drinking it on ice. This is not sake but shochu that they are drinking.

Shochu, heaven or hell? That depends...

I once introduced a good friend to the drink of shochu, explaining one of its greatest attributes is that it doesn't give me a hangover. After a night out of sampling different types of the drink, we called a close and headed back to our hotel. In the morning my friend, a large sports fan and one of the fittest people I know, arrived at the reception looking something akin to death warmed up. Looking very pointedly at me he recounted that I'd said shochu doesn't give you a hangover. I countered that I'd actually said it doesn't give *me* a hangover and I was feeling fine. He wasn't happy.

Shochu is an acquired taste but very popular coming in three basic types. There are varieties based on rice, barley or potato and then these break into different varieties as with sake. Be a little careful though when you first start to drink shochu, try filling your glass with ice first and letting the ice melt as you drink. Shochu is very refreshing but a lot stronger than sake, typically 25% or in some cases 40%. A few glasses and you're going to feel this. It's also a wonderful base for summer drinks, lemonade with a shot of shochu in it and lots of ice is perfect for a hot humid summer afternoon. There is also an urban myth surrounding shochu that it is extremely low in cholesterol and therefore one of the healthier drinks to enjoy. My medical friends assure me this is completely unfounded but it does provide a good excuse in case you need one.

Crying – how do children's cartoons cry?

In Western countries, a child will typically draw someone crying with tears running down the face from the inside corner of the eye and down the side of the nose. Not in Japan. Here the image would be for the tears to run down from the outer corner of the eye and down the side of the face. If you see someone holding a finger to the outer corner of their eye and wiping it down the side of their face they're indicating that they were crying or sad. You won't see someone motioning down the side of their nose though, and you probably won't be understood if you do this either.

Slicing and dicing and the waving hand

You are probably used to the situation where, when trying to work your way through a crowd of people, you find yourself continuously saying "excuse me" as you have to push past someone or end up having to walk through the middle of a conversation. Here you'll see someone, rather than saying excuse me, silently chop the air in front of themselves with their hand as if it were a knife. Although at first this may seem a little uncalled for, it's actually a very polite gesture, called tegatana (hand sword) that is both asking your permission to come through and apologizing at the same time. Historically, in addition to this, the proponent of this gesture was also demonstrating that they were not carrying a weapon and therefore not a threat.

Driving on the left – unless you're in a Mercedes

Japan drives on the left. Interestingly though, foreign cars with left hand drive are actually relatively common and seen as something of an unspoken status symbol. This has been taken to such an extent that exit barriers in the more upmarket hotels will actually have pay stations on both sides of the car to accommodate this.

The one exception to driving on the left is pre-1974 Okinawa. Okinawa was the last province of Japan to be returned to Japanese rule subsequent to the war. As it was effectively an American protectorate, it matched the US system and people drove on the right. Upon returning to Japanese rule this was reversed and Okinawa became one of the few places in the world to switch from driving on the right to driving on the left.

Omi-ai, the journey to find your life partner

In a certain sense, an omi-ai could be considered an arranged marriage. However, it isn't quite that. Omi-ai could be translated as "to look for love" and is a traditional system of introducing couples to each other but then leaving it up to them to see where the relationship goes. It should more be considered a blind date organized by an "introducer" but one where both parties are ultimately looking for marriage and so someone looking for a more casual relationship wouldn't be considered appropriate for an introduction.

Traditionally the introducers play a very important role in the future lives of the couple. If a wedding results from an omi-ai then it will often be the people who introduced the couple who will be at the top table and the parents relegated to a secondary position.

It's actually quite a practical system in the current day and age of busy lives and long working hours. Someone's manager may know someone who they think would be a good match and introduce the two knowing they are both looking to settle down. The couple will meet, usually for dinner, and see if they like each other. As it's such an important decision though it's common for couples to have many such arranged meetings, perhaps as many as thirty or forty separate introductions, until they find the right person and decide to settle down.

Join a go-kon and meet three for the price of one

The go-kon, or "polite conversation" is a more modern variant on the idea of an omi-ai, however without the formal introductory couple. Again the underlying purpose of a go-kon is to find a husband or wife however they tend to be much more casual in nature than an omi-ai and arranged by the individuals themselves. To do this the format is usually three men and three women. One of the couples will know each other and invite two friends to make up the numbers. As the purpose is to find a serious relationship, even though the evening is fun, it's understood by all that they are looking for something serious. Married people are obviously not invited and although they can be the ones to arrange the evening in the first place, it's uncommon for them to join.

If you work in a casual office and are in the position of applying for a new job with another company there is always the problem of explaining why you're wearing a suit to the office that day. The Go-kon is the perfect answer to this. When people ask why you're wearing a suit just smile and say "go-kon". If you're single they'll laugh and wish you luck, if you're married they'll smile and know not to ask any more.

Obon – not actually a holiday

The Obon holidays usually fall in the second week of August. They aren't actually national holidays but almost everyone will take the time off as it's a family time where people will return to their home towns and remember their ancestors, especially if there has been a bereavement during the year. On many lakes across the country people will launch small paper boats with candles burning in memory of a lost loved on and if you get the chance, it is something to quietly witness.

Although Obon is not actually a national holiday, this doesn't prevent the major cities from emptying out. The Shinkansen will run at over 300% capacity on the peak days and the highways will become traffic jams snaking over half the country. It is not uncommon at these times to hear news reports of stationary traffic with tailbacks over 100 kilometers (sixty miles) long.

The simple solution is don't travel at these times. However, if you have to, be careful about your timing. The Japan highway authority will issue in advance traffic warnings of when peaks are expected. And the surprising thing is, they are always right. Although people know they are driving into a major traffic jam, they still do it year in, year out. However, the difference between sitting in stationary traffic and driving along an empty highway can be a simple matter of a few hours. Leave before or after the peak and your travel will be quite normal.

One issue to be aware of is organizing any kind of company event during the Obon week. Head offices outside Japan are unlikely to know about Obon and your Japanese staff will be too polite to mention it if something is organized at this time. But no one will thank you for it and you should have recognized this is equivalent to calling a mandatory department meeting on Christmas day in the West. Many companies close and provide staff an extra two days paid vacation but in case yours doesn't, it is a good idea to ensure that staff are as free as possible at this time and even encourage them to take the time off anyway and spend it with the family. They will appreciate the gesture even if they stay firmly rooted to their desks.

Golden Week – a fortunate accident

Golden Week is the time at the end of April and beginning of May when four national holidays fall closely together. Starting on 29 April with Showa day and ending on 5 May with Children's Day, the weekend can sometimes fall so that it is possible to take an extended nine-day vacation with only two days actually off work.

Children's Day is a special event in its own right that is celebrated for a number of weeks in advance of the actual day. You will see windsocks or kite-like fish hanging from rooftops and being displayed in public parks all around the country. Anyone with a young child will usually also display the fish outside their house as a wish for the happiness of their child in the future. The fish are called koinobori (literally carp streamer) and range in size and colorfulness. Some can be very large measuring several meters (yards) long however a typical set would be one each for the father and mother and then one for each child (traditionally, although it is known as Children's Day, only boys were celebrated however, these days, this tends to include all children, boys and girls alike) reducing in size and each of a different color. Although the streamers are usually flown from a pole with a spinning vane on top, it is quite legitimate, and much simpler, just to fasten the koinobori to a rope and fasten this to your house. Just remember the order that the longest streamers are at the top and reduce in size to the smallest at the bottom.

Happy Mondays – the three day weekend

Although sometimes it seems that Japan has more national holidays than actual workdays, this isn't quite the case. There are fifteen national holidays celebrating such things as National Greenery Day, the vernal and autumnal equinoxes, Respect for the Aged Day and National Foundation Day. If a holiday falls on a Sunday, in many cases, it is automatically moved to the following Monday (this is quaintly known as "the Happy Monday System") and if two holidays fall a day apart, the day between them is also automatically changed to a holiday. This rarely happens but is possible in both May and September.

If you are planning to travel at these times, be aware that a few days flexibility can make all the difference. During Golden Week, Obon and the New Year holidays, travel is not only much more difficult but also significantly more expensive than at other times of the year. A few days can save a lot off the cost of a plane flight and mean much shorter queues at the airport. If you can move your dates, do.

Gambarimasu – a polite way to say "no"

The actual meaning of *gambarimasu* is "to try one's best". It's a phrase heard throughout society in Japan and is often the final line of the sentence in a conversation. When asked to do something out of the normal the answer will very often be "gambarimasu". The error to avoid though, is to assume that it actually means "yes". The usual meaning in a conversation with a foreigner is "not a chance". It's a more polite way to say it though.

The Narita Divorce

Narita is, as most will already know, the main international airport servicing the capital. The Narita Divorce (*Narita rikon*) occurs when a young couple, probably on honey moon, return from their vacation. It's the first time the guy has been away from his home without his mother to help him, he may have been on the phone to her each day and would have been generally useless, never having looked after himself. Landing back at Narita the new bride decides she's made an awful mistake, turns to her husband and says "sayonara baby!" The Narita divorce.

Genji Monogatari – the Tale of Genji

The Tale of Genji is considered by many to be the first real novel ever written in the world. Penned in the early 11th century, it was actually written by one of the ladies of court to entertain the other ladies. It is an excellent romp across the life of the son of the Emperor and was written over many years as an ongoing cycle. Although many stories and texts existed at the time, The Tale of Genji stands out due to its quality and complexity and hence is often ascribed to be the world's first novel.

Crime in Japan – more likely a foreigner

There is very little low level crime in Japan such as theft, vandalism or assault. Murder tends to be largely within either family, organized crime or the mildly deranged. With gun availability very restricted there tends not to be the large-scale massacres seen in some other countries although knife crime can sometimes be problematic. For example in 2008, a young man ran riot in the Akihabara district of Tokyo stabbing to death eight people. Perversely he was officially arrested on *suspicion* of *attempted* murder. This was a man with a bloody knife in his hand and eight victims around him. I never understood why he wasn't arrested simply for murder itself.

The reason for the generally low level of crime is not only cultural but also partly due to the system of the family register. This is the document that notes, births, deaths, marriages, addresses and other details but it also records criminal convictions and therefore the social sanction to even minor crimes can be quite extreme as a public record of the misdemeanor is with the individual effectively for life.

However, if the crime is worth risking the punishment, Japan is a relatively normal country. Politicians regularly are cited having accepted "loans" and notable business people are indicted for insider trading or tax evasion the same as in any other country. White collar crime though, remains relatively tolerated, recently demonstrated where the culprits of a billion dollar fraud at Olympus were handed suspended jail sentences where as in the West it would have been several years of prison time.

If you find yourself in the unfortunate position of being accused of a crime, for example being caught up in a bar fight late at night, it is important you clarify and demonstrate your innocence before the police commence any paperwork. Once the paperwork has been started, no matter the nature of the accusation, it will be continued to completion.

The one area where Japan does differ significantly from other countries is in the processing of a conviction. The conviction rate in the courts is close to 100% and mostly this is based on confession. In

2012 this came to a head when the police extracted confessions from four separate people in a case of computer hacking before the actual culprit was apprehended. The reason why four separate people confessed to a crime they didn't commit is that in Japan the police can hold you without charge for over three weeks effectively depriving you of contact with the world or even legal representation. At this point most people confess due to the strain of isolation whether they are guilty or not.

This is currently a topic for debate within Japanese society as it is seen as being an area for significant abuse (as the computer hacking scandal clearly demonstrated). If, in the tragic instance you are accused of a crime you did not commit and find yourself in a police holding cell for an extended period of time, do not sign anything unless you are clear you understand its content and agree with it. There have been many cases of foreigners signing false confessions and once this is done, conviction is virtually guaranteed.

The trial processes until recently was restricted to trial by three qualified judges however, in some instances, this has now been extended to three judges plus six *lay judges*. A lay judge is similar in concept to a juror although they are allowed to ask questions and assess the degree of remorse the individual shows for the crime (remembering that most convictions are based on confession). The element of remorse is seen as a key aspect of the sentencing process and those *showing* a greater degree of remorse will often receive a lighter sentence than those who do not. Note, showing remorse is important, actually being remorseful is not necessarily the same issue.

Due to the process of requiring three judges, the due process of law can be somewhat drawn out with a murder case taking many years to come to completion. For example, the trial of the leader of the Aum Shinrikyo cult that was responsible for the sarin gas attack on the Tokyo subway in 1995, commenced with his detainment later that year and continued until 2004. He remains on death row.

Japan retains the death penalty for murder and treason and each year a number of people are executed by hanging. Death row inmates are not told in advance of their execution date and are simply led from their cell to the gallows without ceremony. This is also an area that has brought international criticism however is not under review at this time.

The salaryman – the sacrificial lamb

Businessmen in Japan are referred to as *salarymen*, a distinction made not only to identify they are salaried employees rather than temporary labor, but more as a near badge of honor. Although it is something of a stereotype, office workers will be seen late into the evening working at their desks and joining colleagues for a drink after work before catching the late train home to the family. His (as it predominantly remains the preserve of men in

Japan) life will be seen as a hard one where he is essentially sacrificing himself for the good of the company and, consequently, society as a whole.

In some instances this sacrifice can actually take on a literal meaning. *Karoshi* is the word for "death by overwork" and sadly each year there are a number of cases reported however the true extent to which some people may be working past the point of exhaustion on a regular, if not daily, basis is far in excess of what is officially recorded.

Although the salaryman will nominally live at home with his family, the work hours, late nights and early trains on a long commute, can often mean that they don't actually see their families at all during the week, having arrived home after they have retired to bed and leaving for work before the family rises. Weekends are often the only time a salaryman can relax with his family however he is often too tired to enjoy himself.

The life of a salaryman, it has to be said, is not an easy one.

Japanese years – a new Emperor, a new year

Although Japan has adopted the Western calendar in many instances, it still uses the ancient system of assigning a new era starting with year one, as a new emperor assumes the throne, for official purposes. As I write I have just renewed my driving license, which lasts for five years and will be valid until Heisei 30, this being Heisei 25 or 2013.

Although based on the historical Chinese system, prior to 1868 and the commencement of the Meiji period, the start of a new era was a decision made by the imperial court and so had a certain randomness to it. With the commencement of the Meiji period the system of eras has been formalized and is now based on this approach of a new era starting with the ascension to power of a new emperor.

Each era is named in accordance with the new emperor's title, as has been the tradition since the Meiji Era commenced in 1868. There have been three eras subsequent to the Meiji period; Taisho, Showa and Heisei. As the year can commence at any time within the calendar year, and has so far not been 1 January, certain years can have two designations. 1912 for instance, is both Meiji 45 and Taisho 1 and although this practice has been in place for nearly 150 years, it was only actually enacted into law in 1979.

Telling the time in old Japan

Even the time can be different in Japan. Until the intervention of the twenty-four hour clock, the Japanese time system had twelve "hours" in a day. However, these were not equal in length but rather reserved six hours for daylight and six hours for nighttime. This produced the obvious problem that, as the length of the day changes throughout the year, clocks would need constant adjustment to remain accurate. This became the role of the local priest to ensure all clocks were appropriately adjusted and the image of the priest running from house to house in a village is actually derived from this practice in ancient time.

Midnight – when exactly?

Although midnight is a relatively simple concept, 12 o'clock in the middle of the night, it has been interpreted in Japan to mean the *middle portion of the night*. If someone says they worked until midnight, they're actually saying they worked until some time between around 10.00PM and 3.00AM. In fact, as they didn't say the actual time in this case, it's more probably they worked until around 10.00 than any time much later as they would probably want to claim the credit if they did indeed work later.

Confusion arises as this opens the usage of midnight up to many more instances than under the conventional meaning. Many things now happen at, or during, "midnight" and you can start to be quite impressed at the extent of activity that actually happens at this specific time. If someone tells you that something will happen at "midnight" it's always a good idea to clarify the actual meaning. Do they mean "midnight", or "midnight".

Radio – the daily fix before iPods

Entertainment radio is thin on the ground in Japan and although there are a few excellent stations for music, there's very little in the way of English language commentary, drama or analysis. Also, the frequencies used tend to be different to other countries so if you're thinking of packing your favorite radio, check first, it might not work here at all (something I sadly found after my colleagues in London gave me a wonderful radio as a leaving present).

Turning across the FM dial this afternoon, there are only a handful of channels available however, each major metropolitan area has at least one radio station with bilingual broadcasters. It's important you know which one it is and have a radio that can pick it up. Not necessarily for the music, but these stations were created, under a new law following the Kobe Earthquake in 1995, to be the emergency channels for non-Japanese speakers. Although the Internet remained working in Tokyo following the 2011 earthquake, that was not the case further north in the Tohoku region where there was widespread damage to infrastructure. If a major earthquake did occur in Tokyo, it is probable that radio will be one of the few sources of information in the immediate aftermath.

Following the 2011 earthquake there are now very good hand wind torch/phone charger/radio combined units available these days. One of the first things that sold out in convenience stores on the day of the earthquake itself was batteries and emergency chargers for mobile phones. Having the ability to listen to the radio and recharge a phone using a hand wound charger is a good thing in a crisis.

Police Boxes – the friendly neighborhood *koban*

Throughout the metropolitan cities of Japan are distributed *koban* (police boxes) every few hundred meters. So the story goes, you are never more than five minutes from a policeman. Japan has taken an approach of genuine community policing and the police box is an essential element to not only assisting in deterring and preventing crime but also in helping people with directions or looking after lost property until the owner comes to reclaim it.

The box itself is essentially a small home-office with police business on the ground floor and living quarters on the second. They aren't too luxurious as the footprint will be the size of a single room however policeman in the box will be assigned to it for a number of years and will be well known within the community. The advantage of this distributed system is of course availability with a policeman being effectively present twenty-four hours a day.

The other important issue about police boxes is that they tend to act as a geographical marker for everyone. With the complexities of the addressing system, the police box becomes something of a local landmark and is used as a guide when giving directions. A taxi driver is unlikely to know a specific address but may well know the local koban and be able to drop you there, when you can then ask more specific directions.

Seasons of the year

There are officially the four normal seasons in Japan however they are unofficially augmented by a fifth, rainy season. Rainy season is officially reported in the news and you'll hear announcements such as "rainy season started today in Kyushu". I've never worked out how you define the start of rainy season but it officially starts and finishes in a rolling flow from south to north.

Rainy season comes between spring and summer however often there doesn't seem to be a significant increase in the rainfall. Indeed, as I write this section, rainy season has already begun in Tokyo and yet I am sitting outside under a beautiful clear blue sky.

There is also another use of the four main seasons. It is one of the standard pieces of small talk used by Japanese people to fill the silence. The question is often posed as to whether your home country also has four seasons and although this seems to be a statement of basic lack of understanding of global weather patterns, it is in effect, simply a polite way to keep the conversation moving.

Takyubin – delivery by sprinting trolley

Takyubin is a highly developed private delivery service. They will deliver anything and have even taken customer service to the level of introducing freezer trucks for perishable goods. They don't just deliver envelopes and parcels. And they deliver everything quickly and if you're not in, will leave a note to let you know they called and when you call them back, you can choose the time you'd like them to re-visit to within a two-hour time gap so you know when to be in. They even include the driver's mobile phone number. I marvel every time I compare this to the UK where I was once told my new washing machine would be delivered "next week".

In addition to this they will not only deliver your orders from Amazon to your door, they will also collect payment in the instance you don't like using credit cards across the Internet.

Takyubin is also involved if you go skiing or playing golf. Instead of carrying your skis or clubs onto the train and fighting through the crowds, you can simply take them to your local convenience store and have them delivered from there to the reception of your club, resort or hotel the next day. It's absolutely reliable, very reasonably priced and fast. The only drawback is that you can only deliver items within Japan!

Convenience Stores – how to pay your bills

Convenience stores are everywhere in Japan, selling everything from food and alcohol to paperclips and razor blades. Almost all will sell beer and wine and these days most also have ATMs (cash machines) though, as of the time of writing, these were predominantly in Japanese without an option of English (one chain currently has a button for English which flashes the message "English Not Available" when you press it). The food won't be of the highest quality but if you simply need to restock quickly, they're extremely useful.

Convenience stores are open 24/7 but also provide more services than simple daily supplies. They are also a place where you can pay your utility bills (provided it's not a red demand, for that you'll need to go to the utility provider), pay for your Amazon shipment and drop off your golf clubs for shipment to the next day's tournament. The other thing about most convenience stores is they'll have a public bathroom available if you happen to find yourself in need of one.

The main convenience store chains are 7/11 (now rebranded *7&I* following the acquisition of Ito Yokado by 7/11 and a disagreement over the subsequent name resulting in one of the more interesting compromises in branding history), AM/PM, Family Mart and Lawson's. There are many others though and all provide the same basic services. You will also see long lines of teenagers reading the manga comic books to kill time. Sometimes, they should probably just go home.

Love Hotels for those intimate moments

Japanese houses have traditionally been quite small, often with few rooms and paper-thin walls throughout. A family would typically all sleep together in the same room rather than in separate bedrooms and as a result there is little privacy growing up.

The question then arises about those intimate moments between a married couple and the solution is the entire industry of Love Hotels. These are typically anonymous although usually with a creative and explanatory name that leaves little question as to the purpose of the establishment. They are though, very much a "bring your own" system and are designed to provide an opportunity for a little privacy for a couple away from the family.

Unlike a more conventional hotel, Love Hotels usually offer two alternative prices if you would prefer to "rest" or "stay", the stay referring to staying overnight. The purpose of their existence being to provide a little escapism, the rooms are also often themed and might have a karaoke or Hawaiian theme, mirrors all around or costumes for dressing up. They offer a little fun and privacy and judging by the number of them on the back streets of most towns and cities in Japan, they seem to be very successful at providing just that.

I was once asked by someone from the European head office of the company I was working for if it was normal for hotels in Japan to charge by the hour. They were coming on a visit and had arranged their own accommodation rather than asking the local office to assist. I should have explained about the love hotel system and that may be they would like to transfer to something more conventional but decided it might be an interesting experience for them and so, I said "yes".

Mobile phones – it'll even work outside Japan

For many years, Japan used an international mobile phone standard only available in Japan. This meant that when you travelled, there were no such problems as roaming charges, your phone simply didn't work. The same was true for people visiting Japan, their phones didn't work either. In our company I used to keep half a dozen Japanese handsets on standby for international visitors who found themselves stranded without a working phone. Fortunately, the introduction of 3G slowly put an end to this. Japanese phones worked overseas and foreign phones worked in Japan. As long as you have a 3G phone you'll now be fine. Current (at the time of writing) generation of BlackBerrys also will work in Japan though earlier models simply refused to fire up.

If you are staying for any period of time you'll need to have a locally based mobile phone. All the normal smartphones are available plus the vast array of

Japan specific models. These come in a myriad of designs and styles (including having the ability to hang things from them, something considered important especially by Japanese women). These phones are fine but you probably should confirm that the menu can be switched to English before you purchase one. Most phones you can, but having the person in the store do this for you will save a lot of time and effort later.

The headache of the Yasakuni Shrine

The Yasakuni shrine is one of the major shrines in Tokyo and, similar to many places of dedication around the world, is considered to enshrine the souls of millions of war dead from the time of the Meiji restoration until the end of World War II. Until 1978 this was not considered controversial and, with state and religion being separate within the constitution, there were essentially no political controversies around government ministers visiting the shrine annually to pay their respects.

In 1978 this changed when fourteen Class A war criminals were also added to the enshrinement. From this point onward, attending the shrine to honor the two and a half million who had fought and died for the Emperor also means paying respects to the fourteen individuals condemned and recognized as war criminals. Countries around Asia were horrified that the Japanese government would even consider such a form of recognition and have ever since demanded that government ministers cease to pay homage at the shrine. However the government continues to attend and to cite that, as the shrine is a private memorial, there is nothing the government can do to have the fourteen souls removed. And so, in spring each year, ministers attend and the relationship with Japan's Asian neighbors takes a turn for the worse.

The response of the government, that it is a private shrine and therefore beyond their control, is technically correct if somewhat disingenuous. The shrine is private and therefore the decision to remove the fourteen souls in question is one for the owner who's position is that, once included, it is hard to disentangle and individual soul from the rest and therefore they must stay. However, as has been pointed out many times over the years, there is nothing to prevent the government designating a new, national monument to represent those who fell with honor in the conflicts of the country and visit this to pay their respects instead. Indeed there already is a separate national shrine though it remains sadly under utilized.

History, and whatever happened to 1933 – 1945?

Although I am generalizing, it is not stretching the point too far to say that history is taught in Japanese schools chronologically starting with the Pliocene era through to 1933 in detail, then there may be a few sentences which in summary will say "and then there was a dark period" and then America dropped the bomb with no rhyme, reason or justification.

The war and pre-war period is simply not taught to children in Japan and as a result the post-war generation has a lot of difficulty understanding why their Asian neighbors find it hard to forgive and forget. People simply don't know what they are supposed to be forgiving or forgetting. They never knew it in the first place.

The difference between Japan and Germany arises from the origins and reasons for the war. In Germany, the war was waged, driven and fought by and on behalf of a political belief that was eventually not only destroyed but shown to be something destitute of any good and the very people themselves who had fought for it recognized it should never have arisen in the first place. Germany can look back on its past and analyze what went wrong from the cold detachment of a new generation.

Japan didn't have this opportunity available to detach themselves from their own history. The war had been fought in the name of the Emperor, and until 1945 the Emperor was a living god, descended over two and a half thousand years from the Sun God, Amaterasu, who founded the nation in 660 BC.

The issue being that the Emperor was still emperor after the war. To criticize the objectives and execution of the war would be to directly criticize the Emperor, something the country was simply not willing or able to conceive or consider. And so to move forward and allow the country to peacefully rebuild and recover, a national decision was taken to simply forget what had happened. The war was not discussed or taught and the country could find peace of mind.

The concern here is that it has led to tensions and misunderstandings with Japan's neighbors who see the war in a very different light. This isn't going to be resolved any time soon or may be at all, but it all derives from the decision that it was preferable at the time to keep the Emperor in place to hold the very fragile country together than to remove him and risk a complete breakdown. For good or ill, the decision brought peace and stability and eventually lifted millions from poverty and into prosperity.

The issue is not helped by the occasional ministerial statement that is not only wildly inaccurate but a continuous reminder to Japan's neighbors that the country is having difficulty coming to terms with the past. A little bit of diplomacy on the subject would go a long way. For example, an ex-foreign minister was surprised to know that the League of Nations didn't, in fact, authorize the annexation of Korea in 1910, mainly because it hadn't been created until 1919.

The Pacifist Constitution – written in English

The Japanese constitution is one of the few national documents that can be read in English and completely understood without having to be concerned about translational nuances or cultural differences. This is because it was written by an

American team working under McArthur, in a little over three days and presented to the Japanese delegation complete and finished.

McArthur's team at the time had been trying to implement a series of key issues in the constitution but with the objective of having the Japanese delegation write it themselves. However, each draft by the Japanese team was essentially the same one, the Emperor ruled by divine right and that was the end of the discussion. Eventually McArthur lost patience and instructed his team to write it themselves, which they did in a matter of days and then he simply presented it to the Japanese delegation. At first there was some confusion as the delegation thought this was a discussion document until McArthur simply said no, this is the new constitution.

The document rejected the concept of belligerency to settle disputes between nations and renounced the right to armed forces of any kind (although this has been re-interpreted over the years as being "offensive" armed forces, Japan having one of the largest defense budgets in Asia). Additionally, the constitution also guaranteed equal rights for women, something that hadn't been a discussion point prior to the American occupation. But in 1947 there it was, the new constitution, written in English, for Japan. And it remains unchanged, without amendment, to this day.

Navigation systems – marriage preservation

Almost all cars you can buy in Japan will come with an on-board navigation (navi) system these days. The systems are currently more advanced than in many other countries as they also indicate the traffic situation on almost all roads and highways and can automatically re-route you around traffic jams and general hot spots.

Many non-Japanese cars sold in Japan may also have the option to switch the menus for the navigation system into English, however there are no options to actually switch the maps themselves into English. It simply wouldn't be economically viable to have both a Japanese and an English set of maps, the requirement being 99.9% for the Japanese version 0.1% for the English.

Navi systems not only provide real time traffic information for almost all roads in Japan but they also allow you to search for a destination by address, phone number, direct location on a map as well as allowing you to select to show car parks, fast food restaurants or gasoline stations for example. There are literally dozens of ways to find your destination by browsing through the touch screen menu. And none of them involves an argument.

Maps on the subway walls – and tenement halls

If you've ever found yourself confused and disoriented after looking at the large maps on the walls in subways, you're not alone. The key issue here is that, unlike in almost any other country, North is not necessarily at the top. The map is oriented in a way that you would view the ground in front of you if the earth were transparent. So if you find yourself lost and walking in circles, you're certainly not on your own.

Taxes – there's no avoiding them

Costs in Japan could be considered relatively high in comparison to other countries in the world and taxes are no exception. All residents, which also includes those who have recently arrived but have the *intention* of staying longer than one year, are liable for two sets of income tax.

National income tax is paid directly to the Japanese government and in addition to this, local inhabitant tax is paid to the municipal government. At the time of writing this could add up in total to a marginal tax rate of 50%. And that is before social insurance.

Anyone earning in excess of ¥20 million per year must file a tax return with the local tax office. There are many outsourcing companies that can assist in this and as the forms are all required to be filed in Japanese, this is a useful value added service. There are all the usual international tax advisory firms that can assist in reducing a tax exposure, there being no laws saying you must pay the maximum tax, however, all advice will of course come with a fee.

One reason many international firms employ expatriate staff outside Japan and second them into the country is not to avoid or evade tax but to reduce the burden of social insurance. If you are employed by a Japanese company, to all intents and purposes you have no option but to pay social insurance contributions. However, if you are employed outside Japan, this is not the case and the combined savings for company and individual are approximately 20% of the cost of employment. The reason for doing this is that these contributions are towards medical insurance and a retirement pension. As an expatriate is unlikely to need either of these, it does make sense to offshore the employment.

Yakuza – the other side of society

The yakuza in Japan are these days akin to the concept of the Mafia in America. Although not formed around family ties, they are tight knit crime syndicates that have historical backgrounds originating during the Edo period from groups of gamblers and peddlers that today consider themselves to be members of a more "noble" organization.

There are over 90,000 yakuza members in Japan, a reasonably accurate figure as they also are *required to register with the police* and so the groups are known and membership openly recognized. The largest syndicate is the Yamaguchi-gumi that is based in Kobe, Western Japan, though with growing influence in Tokyo.

The yakuza are involved in all forms of organized crime across Japan and also branch out into other areas of Asia. The most common time you may come across yakuza will be on the streets of Ginza or Roppongi where you'll be able to recognize them with tight curled hair and dark glasses usually driving a Mercedes or other left hand drive foreign luxury brand automobile.

However, they do not usually interact with foreigners and so if you ignore them, they will also ignore you. Companies are occasionally contacted by yakuza and encouraged to make "community support" payments. In this instance there are specialists who can be called upon to manage the situation and minimize any disruption.

The yakuza are also responsible for the peculiarity that almost all listed companies in Japan hold their Annual Shareholder Meetings on the same day as each other. One way for yakuza to historically extort funds from companies was to find embarrassing information about a company or the directors and then threaten to ask awkward questions at the meeting unless a contribution is made to their funds. This led the companies to hold their meetings on the same day so that they can't all suffer this disruption as there are too many meetings for all of them to be attended. It is also now illegal for the companies themselves to make payments to yakuza as a result of this form of encouragement. The other option would obviously be to stop doing anything illegal or embarrassing.

The yakuza see themselves as more than simple crime organizations though. On the morning of January 17, 1995, the Great Hanshin Earthquake leveled the city of Kobe slightly before 6.00AM. It was after lunch time that the Japanese government was informed and not until later that day did they organize "training" flights over the city to assess the damage as the violence of the earthquake had been so extreme as to disable all sensor networks and so in Tokyo people were essentially blind to what was happening on the ground. The yakuza on the other hand were handing out blankets and food from early in the morning and effectively took over the role of the government emergency agencies in the days that followed.

The money system – notes and coins

Coins are simple in Japan. There are ¥1, ¥5, ¥10, ¥50, ¥100 and ¥500 coins each that clearly displays the number in English on one side. That is except for the ¥5 coin. If you are wondering what the small, bronze colored coin is with a hole in the middle, it's the ¥5 one. It actually does display the denomination clearly on it, however it uses the Japanese symbol for five. All others use Western characters so you'll be able to see these immediately. The other thing about the ¥5 coin is that it's considered somewhat lucky as the pronunciation "go-en" is a similar sound to making a polite bond or relationship. As a result they're often used as the gift at a temple or put into a new wallet to create a connection.

Notes come in ¥1,000, ¥2,000, ¥5,000 and ¥10,000 denominations. However, the ¥2,000 note, when introduced in 2000, proved to be so unpopular that it has effectively been withdrawn from circulation and you are unlikely to come across it unless you specifically request it at a bank.

One final thing about currency, although it is denominated in "yen", when counted it is pronounced in Japanese as "en", so "ten-yen" becomes "ju-en". Although at times it can be difficult to adjust to working in yen compared to other currencies, if you try to pay for a ¥900 taxi ride with a ¥10,000 note, you should remember you've just tried the equivalent of paying a $9 taxi fair with a $100 bill. Don't be surprised if the driver says no.

Manga – what are those comic books about?

Manga are the thick comic books seen everywhere across Japan and seemingly available in any store whether it's a cheap convenience store or a high-end bookshop. Some are of very high quality and the artists are famous for their work. Others are just plain pornographic it has to be said, and probably would fall foul of obscenity laws in many countries.

Here Manga are seen as an escapist art form and are read by nearly everyone from all age groups. I would strongly suggest though that before buying one for children or to send home as a present, you have a quick check of the contents; you don't want any difficult questions from either children or passport control as you return to your country on home leave.

Manga are read everywhere and usually with people around. It is normal to see a middle aged, bespectacled and be-suited salaryman on a train pull out a manga from his briefcase and bury his nose in it to his destination. It is also fairly common for the artwork to be something that would probably make your auntie blush. You will also see youths in convenience stores spending an evening reading manga directly from the rack. The store staff don't mind (it's not their store) and there's always a new edition to read. Though we would probably hold it at arms length turning it around as we take in the depiction.

Hay fever – the annual itch

Post-war, Japan was urgently in need of cheap timber for construction. As a result it embarked on a massive campaign to replant large areas of forest with quick growing cedar. However, over many years the restrictions on import of construction materials were relaxed and it became cheaper to use foreign sourced wood for new buildings than Japanese grown cedar. The upshot of this has been that the cedar, which was planted sixty years ago, is no longer economically viable to harvest and so is simply left to grow. And the bigger a tree grows, the more pollen it produces.

Over the last twenty years this issue has continued to worsen drastically and during February and March the major cities of Japan are brought to a near standstill as the population suffers with ever worsening hay fever. If you are normally a sufferer you'll need your medicine ready and possibly consider air-filters for the house. If you are not normally a sufferer and find yourself with a continuous headache in February, irritated eyes and a blocked nose, *you are now a sufferer* and will be each year around the same time until the government finally decides to take action.

Urushi – Poison Ivy – avoided at all costs

The sap of the urushi tree is prized and collected to make the black lacquer used to coat fine wooden ornaments in Japan. Unfortunately, it is also highly toxic to 80% of people and will bring out an allergic reaction similar to extreme poison ivy. The rashes can split the skin and bleed and are extremely painful and will last several weeks in severe cases. If you see an urushi plant simply leave it alone, don't try to dig it up and don't try to burn it as the smoke can be fatal and it will do to your lungs the same the sap did to your skin. Fortunately, urushi plants are fairly easy to recognize with the distinctive red color to their stems. You will not find these plants within the city but you may if you go hiking in the mountains. Simply leave them alone.

If you do come into contact with an urushi plant and realize it at the time, you have approximately fifteen minutes to wash the sap thoroughly off your skin (whilst trying to not to spread it further). Simply wash with soap and water and you may be able to remove it completely. After this time the toxin has bonded with your skin and cannot be removed. At this point you are going to have a reaction (unless you're one of the lucky 20% of people who are immune) and should seek medical treatment. The rash takes two to three days to start and will get worse before it gets better.

If you have had a severe reaction to the urushi plant you should also be careful that in the future you avoid touching any items that may have been coated in the lacquer the oil is used for. Simply touching such items can trigger a secondary reaction as the body responds to what it perceives as a new urushi exposure. Again, if this occurs and a reaction starts, seek medical help to alleviate the worst of the symptoms as best possible.

Bugs, bites and things that slither in the night

The good news is there are no fatally poisonous spiders, insects or snakes on mainland Japan. If you travel to some of the tropical islands near Okinawa you may want to check in advance but on the mainland you're safe. Also on a positive note, there are no serious insect-borne diseases such as malaria or sleeping sickness. There are bugs though.

On the Izu peninsular, a popular weekend vacation area southwest of Tokyo, there are spiders the size of your hand. I'm not good with spiders it has to be said and usually would rather lease them territory than actually deal with one if I find it in my room. They're not poisonous though so if you don't have problems with spiders, they're not an issue for you at all. In the cities you're very unlikely to see any form of spider except for a very small one that hops around and causes no harm.

There are a number of types of snake on the mainland islands and some even find their way into the center of cities. On more than one occasion I've seen long Rat Snakes in Yoyogi Park in the middle of Tokyo. As with the spiders they are not poisonous though and you can simply ignore them and they'll leave you alone.

In the summer months the cicada come out and make an ear piecing noise until the cool of the Autumn sets in. Cicada in Japan are called *semi* and although they are relatively large for an insect, being about the size of your thumb, they are again completely safe. Just very loud and a little intimidating in appearance.

The biggest issue you may have to face from insects are mosquitos. It's interesting that people new to Japan seem to react to them significantly more than they would react to one from their home country. Although I have now become accustomed to mosquito bites, when I first arrived the swelling from a single bite would cover several centimeters and often actually bleed. However, there is a remedy for this. At all drug stores you can buy a little brown bottle called *kinkan*. It's ammonia based (so don't sniff it) and you simply wipe it across a bite. The irritation goes almost instantly and the swelling can be kept under control. Careful putting it on your face though as the fumes will sting your eyes and it shouldn't be used for small children (there are patches that kids can use) as the feeling of the ice cold liquid may upset them. Without kinkan though, life in Japan could have been very unpleasant indeed and, after all these years, I'm still grateful to my friend who first introduced me to it after I'd left a window open one night and was suffering from something close to thirty bites all over me.

There are wasps and bees in the city but this is actually quite rare. It is more of an issue if you are out of the city in the forests. Small wasps tend to swarm and if you see a nest near you, ask for help and don't try to remove them yourself. There is also a large wasp species where a single insect will be around the size of your thumb. These are not aggressive and tend not to swarm however I'm told by people who've experienced it that being stung by one may be the most painful experience of your life. In fact, these large wasps are said to be so painful they can induce anaphylactic shock and, as a result, are responsible for more deaths annually than any other creature in Japan (excluding us). General advice is to try not to get stung by one.

Out of the city centers there is also a fly similar to a horse fly. You often don't notice these and when they bite you may not even feel it. However, the bite will swell and the center will ooze clear liquid for up to two weeks. Once bitten there's almost nothing you can do about this, you can use kinkan but it is going to hurt for a while.

Other animals you may see out of the city

There are over 150 species of mammal alone in Japan so it's unsurprising that from time to time you are going to come across some of them. Add in birds and reptiles and you have quite a collection overall. Generally though, the animals you'll come across in the city and outside the city tend to be different.

Inside cities you'll occasionally see bats swirling in the evening light but the main flying creature you'll see are the large black crows which are typically twice the size of crows in Europe. A previous mayor of Tokyo was once attacked by one and vowed to eliminate them from the city completely. Although he didn't succeed in his endeavors, he did a reasonable job and the crow populations are now lower than before. One point here is to make sure your trash/rubbish is covered either in a strong plastic bin or by a heavy nylon net (Japan doesn't generally use trash cans). If not, you'll find all of last night's dinner spread across the street in front of your house.

Once you're out of the city and into the mountains you have a good chance of seeing quite a range of creatures. Deer are quite common and are not too frightened of people. Watch out at night though as they tend to get caught in car headlights and freeze. If you're on dipped beam you'll need to be quick on the breaks.

There are bears in Japan and very occasionally there will be a report of one being sighted in a town or even attacking someone. This is extremely rare but if you're hiking, make sure you check before you leave if there are bears around in the area. If there are, and you still don't want to change your plans, just be noisy so you don't surprise them. If they hear you coming they'll head in the opposite direction.

One of the both mythical and real creatures of Japan is the tanuki. It's often referred to (incorrectly) as a raccoon but is unrelated to the US raccoon. Raccoon Dog is also used for its name in English but as tanuki is easy to remember and a great sounding word, why not add this one to your vocabulary. In Japanese mythology tanuki often appear as mischievous creatures though somewhat lazy but of a happy go lucky nature. When you see them you can imagine where this reputation came from. You'll generally only see them at night running across a road and at first you might think it a cat but if you're in the forests or mountains there tend not to be any cats so it's more likely a tanuki.

There are no large cats on mainland Japan bigger than the domesticated ones and although there are feral cats in the city, out of town you won't come across any unless it's a pet. On some of the outlying islands there are endangered species of medium size cats but these are very rarely seen.

Wild boar are common in the mountains and the hunting season stretches from November to March. Although you can buy it for BBQ, there is a domesticated wild pig that generally tastes much better if you're planning something. Wild boar are large, intelligent and angry. If you're considering hiking in an area known to have wild boar it's a good idea to ask advice in advance of what to do if you come face to face with one. They are very territorial and are known to attack people especially if surprised.

There are also monkeys on mainland Japan though mostly found towards the Japan Sea coast and in the mountains of central and northern Japan. Monkeys are highly intelligent and can become aggressive if surprised or approached too closely. Leave them alone and they'll leave you alone too (though they may target your sandwiches!). However, if you are staying in an area known to have monkeys, it's best to close all windows at night, as they are known on occasion to enter into a house looking for food. They are also known to be clever enough to take a plastic shopping bag with them when they raid orchards in search of apples. They've learnt that they can carry a lot more than if they try to pick them up and carry them by hand!

There are also a number of mountain resorts with onsen where monkeys will often come and share the hot water with you. Although this can make for a great photo opportunity, as normal, ask advice first on how close you can go and how tame the monkeys are. Remember that they are a lot stronger than they look.

There are also many species of birds of prey in Japan from falcons to Golden Eagles. These you will see mostly either in the mountains or in some cases on the sea coasts and can have a wing span of up to two meters (six feet). I once had something large land heavily on the roof of the house I was staying at in the mountains only to listen to it devour something smaller and leave parts of it liberally spread all around.

Handguns in Japan – a national approach

Although police in Japan routinely carry handguns, they are not available in any form to the civilian population. It is extremely rare to hear of a gun crime and in 2011, only eight people in the entire country died from gun related activity. There are shooting clubs though and clay pigeon shooting is reasonably accessible if this is a sport you enjoy. On the whole though, you are more likely to be injured by a policeman dropping his gun on you than from any form of actual bullet. Gun crime is simply not within the Japanese mindset and people are very comfortable with this.

Vending machines – no, they don't sell those

Vending machines are everywhere in Japan and offer a remarkable range of products. There are many urban legends around these, though to be honest, the most I've seen in a vending machine is soft drinks or cigarettes. Even beer vending machines seem to be on the decline these days.

There are reputedly over twenty million vending machines on the streets of Japan. Coca Cola alone has over one million vending machines on the streets. And they always work, are never vandalized and are never empty.

In fact I have only once experienced a time when the vending machines of Japan were empty and that was in the days following the earthquake in 2011. Rumors spread through the population in Tokyo that the water supply had been contaminated with radioactive fallout from Fukushima. The rumors were false and rather irresponsible but there was a run on bottled drinks and the vending machines ran dry. For about two days. And then they were all full again and life returned to normal.

Daylight Savings – a serious business

Tampering with the rising sun is a serious business in Japan. Daylight savings is not utilized although it is widely recognized that this would lead to the opportunity for a better quality of life as well as being more energy efficient. The main concern though, that seems to kill off the discussion, is the feeling of obligation Japanese workers feel to their companies.

In government research, the main issue is the potential to actually negatively impact the quality of life and that people would stay longer in the office rather than take advantage of lighter evenings. One quote that summed this up that appeared in the press was from a man who said "I just don't think I can go home in daylight".

Speaker Vans – something to avoid

As an overarching generalization, Japan is a quiet and peaceful place. And then there are the speaker vans. These are trucks and buses, painted black with right wing slogans written across them, that drive the streets of the main cities with huge speakers mounted on top screaming essentially war time rhetoric to everyone passing by. Best advice, if you see one coming, head in the opposite direction, they are very, very loud and there's nothing you're going to be able to do about them. The good news is that they only come out occasionally and on special days (National Foundation Day is a favorite) so you won't come across them too often. Every country has its political right wing and this is Japan's.

Why are ten people standing by the road works?

When I first arrived in Japan I couldn't believe the cost of everything and then I couldn't believe the mass inefficiency of the country. This wasn't the super smooth robot like machine I'd read about and expected to see. Everywhere I looked there were women polishing escalator hand rails, men with red batons telling me to watch out for the huge and very well illuminated road works, girls in the elevators explaining what the sign (helpfully in English in some department stores) said and generally an entire workforce performing what in reality were non-jobs.

My initial reaction, as for many people I believe, was that if Japan eliminated all of this under-employment, costs would fall and prices would too as a result. A very simple solution or so I thought. However on closer examination there is more to this than meets the eye. Compared to many Western countries, Japan has very limited social security support. If you are out of work your benefits last a few months at best and there is no such thing as long term unemployment benefit. The family is typically expected to support a family member out of work but, as a society as a whole, everyone sees it as part of their responsibility as well. By providing these seemingly unnecessary roles, the nation is essentially saying that it is willing to support each individual and take the consequences through higher prices.

You can look at this in simple terms if you consider that in Western countries we often pay benefits to individuals so that they can stay at home and be unproductive. In Japan there is an accepted national cost to paying a benefit for these people to continue to work irrespective of the productivity of that work. The big difference being, in Japan the person still gets up in the morning, gets ready for work and does their job as best they can. They still have the self-respect of doing something no matter what that something is. I changed my opinion on this one in Japan after a little thought and these days enjoy the feeling of humanity this brings. Not everything is about the money.

Why do we call Japan, Japan? – ask Marco Polo

One of the first things you'll notice after you arrive is that Japan is not called Japan but Nippon (or Nihon in certain circumstances). Nippon translates from the kanji as "the origin of the sun" and hence the familiar "land of the rising sun" description often used outside Japan. The reason why Westerners refer to Japan as "Japan" though, is thought to relate back to the travels of Marco Polo. Although he didn't come to Japan itself, he spent over twenty years travelling China and other countries in the east. He learnt the Chinese name for Nippon and hence when he returned to Europe, Marco Polo told of stories of a land across the sea that everyone in China called "Japan".

Japanese ghosts - don't swim in lakes

There are as many ghost stories in Japan as anywhere else. However, you will always be able to recognize a Japanese ghost as it will have a long neck and no feet. Never understood this one. Ghosts and evil spirits haunt lakes and still water so the idea of taking a dip in the local pond to cool off is not generally considered a good idea. Rivers fine, lakes not. There is probably historical reasons for this as typically moving water doesn't carry disease to the same extent as static pools, so when in Rome, bathe in a river.

Japanese excel at inventing and telling ghost stories. If you ever have the chance to watch either The Grudge or The Ring you will see what I mean. I'd also recommend you watch them in daylight. Although many Japanese horror movies have been remade in English, you will tend to find that the better ones work just as well, if not more so, in the original Japanese. Even if you don't understand a word, you will definitely get the point.

Volcanoes – and there are many of them

Japan is a volcanic island and there's a reason why it's said to be on "The Ring of Fire". They do erupt every now and then. The last major eruption was Mt Unzen on the southern island of Kyushu in 1991 which took the lives of 43 people, however there are smaller ones every few years. In 2005 Mount Asama had a minor eruption but still put dust onto Tokyo 200 kilometers (120 miles) away.

Just to reassure the reader, volcanic eruptions, unlike earthquakes, can be predicted with reasonable accuracy and the active volcanoes across Japan are constantly monitored for signs of life.

Volcanoes produce extremely picturesque mountains and many in Japan closely resemble a child's drawing of what a volcano should look like. However, although many are an enjoyable climb, many are also closed to the public due to the dangers of poison gas. The gas is a natural product of volcanic activity however, in certain circumstances this gas can seep out and collect in ravines and depressions in the land. These are extremely dangerous and often fatal as when you walk into one of the gas pockets, the gas is odorless and the first you will know that you are being suffocated is that you will become dizzy and unable to breath, asphyxiation will result in minutes unless you can reach high ground before being overcome. Before heading out on a hike up a volcano, it's worth confirming that it's open; many don't each year and a number of hikers don't come back.

Will Fuji erupt?

Yes, it's an active volcano, that's what they do. The last eruption was 1707 and since the Tohoku earthquake there has been discussion as to whether it's preparing to erupt again. That may well be the case however, no need to panic yet. It's about 100 kilometers (sixty miles) from Tokyo and there will be major warnings broadcast several days before any action.

If you have friends living in the immediate vicinity of Fuji you may want to give them a call and offer a bed for a few days. If it does erupt, the best viewing in Tokyo includes the view from The Park Hyatt, The Cerulean and Roppongi Hills. If you're not leaving, take the opportunity to witness something spectacular!

Unless something extraordinary happens you should be safe in Tokyo in the event Fuji does go up. Listen to news broadcasts and check the website of your embassy but apart from dust there should be no impact on Tokyo. That is not the case for areas closer to the mountain. Mishima, Gotemba, Hakone and areas around the five lakes are likely to be hit hard. Unfortunately that includes the Shinkansen between Tokyo and Osaka and the main highways.

These major transport routes are likely to be severely disrupted but will have been closed in advance of any actual eruption. Flights will also be affected with planes being diverted away from the area. It is likely that travel between Japan's two largest cities may be via a third country for a while.

Although it is an active volcano, it's possible to climb Fuji in the summer months but if you try outside that time and get into difficulty, you're paying for the rescue. Don't take it lightly, it's 3,776m and the hike from the fifth station is a vertical lift higher than from sea-level to the peak of the highest mountain in the UK.

Living in Japan

Living in Japan will be nothing if not an experience for you. Japanese culture and style is unlike anything elsewhere including the neighboring countries of Asia. Several years living in Singapore will provide scant preparation for your time in Japan.

As with all new countries, the experience can have both positive and negative elements to it and the frustrations can sometimes seem to outweigh the pleasures. The important point to remember is that *you are not the first person to throw your hands in the air and declare "But Why?"*

This section aims to provide advice and guidance on "how to..." when you are actually on the ground in Japan. Some aspects of life may at first appear randomly problematic but in reality there is often (though not always) a logic to what is happening and how a few simple ideas will make life significantly easier.

Learning the language – really, it can be done!

There's a reason why auto-translation systems don't work well with the Japanese language. There are no definitive particles ("the") so an explanation in Japanese is inherently vague. I've been in meetings where I thought it was just me only to find all my colleagues would walk out and say they also didn't follow what was being discussed either. Somehow this doesn't actually make me feel any better.

It took me a few years before I started to dream in Japanese. That's the point at which you know you're comfortable with a language. Slow for someone who is already multilingual, but reasonable for someone who arrived in the country a bilingual illiterate (someone who can't read and write in two languages), like myself. Structure was now fixed in my head and so now it's just a matter of vocabulary. Compared to learning other languages this seems a rather long time however when you start with Japanese you'll encounter three key issues:

1) The grammatical structure is essentially the reverse of English
2) You can't read any of it so practice is limited
3) There's more than one version of "Japanese"

The last of these points is, in reality the key reason why it is more efficient to focus time on learning the cultural aspects of living in Japan as a priority to learning to speak the language for business.

Spoken Japanese comes in multiple versions dependent on whether the speaker is a man or woman and then, to add to the complexity, whether the listener is junior or senior to the speaker themselves. To take an example, depending on circumstances, the Japanese word for "I" could be:

Watakushi – used by men and women to be very polite,
Watashi – used by men and women in normal conversation,
Atashi – used by women only when talking to a friend,
Boku   – used by men when talking to friends,
Ore – used by men when talking to someone more junior.

And they all mean the same thing, "I".

As a result, simply trying to learn standard Japanese becomes the best option but is no guarantee of either understanding a reply or avoiding smiles from everyone around when using the incorrect version. As I can testify to when, having learnt a substantial portion of my Japanese from my wife, smiles breakout when I use a distinctly feminine phrase to the guys in the office.

If you're only coming to Japan for two or three years it's probably not realistic to achieve a business level of fluency this quickly unless you're an outstanding linguist to begin with. Target the simple things that will help make life easier; for example how to direct taxis or order pizza by the phone.

In reality you shouldn't be overly concerned by not aiming to be fluent in the language from an early stage, *learning the culture and recognizing a situation can be a much more rewarding and effective approach than simply trying to memorize vocabulary.* When you understand that a Japanese "yes" could well mean "no" then you're on much safer ground. It still makes me smile when a new foreigner arrives in Japan and after a few weeks tells me it's much easier than they thought as everyone agrees with what they're saying. They're not, but they're happy you think so.

When you do start to use some suitably chosen words also remember that less than 50% of English speakers in the world are native so as a native speaker I'm used to hearing many different versions and mis-pronunciations of the language. 99.9% of Japanese speakers in the world though are native speakers. People are simply not used to hearing errors and this leads to a major difficulty. When a native English speaker hears an error they tend to automatically tune it out and replace the error with the correct word or pronunciation. It's essentially a reflex action not requiring any particular thought or effort. However, when a Japanese person hears incorrect Japanese, they have no experience to fall back on. Most times you will simply receive a blank stare even though the word or pronunciation is so incredibly close. A 5% error does not lead to a 5% misunderstanding. It usually leads to 100% confusion.

You will experience becoming invisible. All conversations will be directed to the person in the group who appears Japanese (whether they are or not). One Chinese colleague of mine used to find this amusing when I would order something in a restaurant in fluent Japanese to have the waitress turn to him and ask what I'd like. To add insult to injury, I'd actually have to explain to him what the waitress was asking. Some find this quite frustrating however don't let it get to you, it's part of life in Japan so you'll need to learn to live with it. Japan isn't going to change any time soon.

When speaking English there are techniques that may help you along. Obviously speak slowly and clearly, place clear breaks between words (but no need to shout, no one's deaf) but also idioms should be avoided as much as possible. "Taking someone under your wing" takes on a whole new meaning when you consider it literally! If the person doesn't understand you the first time, it's helpful to say the same thing exactly the same way a second time even though the natural tendency is to try and say it differently. The person your talking to is doing their best to understand you and is probably translating your words in their head, and if you change the way you're saying something they have to start the process all over again from the beginning.

Learning to Read and Write – all over again

As mentioned, the key to learning Japanese is to set realistic objectives. On a two year assignment, there is essentially no realistic point in setting out to achieve a level of written Japanese to a standard high enough to read a daily newspaper for example. Apart from anything you need not only three new alphabets, but approximately two thousand characters of one of those before even starting on the multiple pronunciations if you aim to read out loud. However there is a lot of benefit to be gained by simply aiming to make life more comfortable in the written language of your host country.

Not being able to read everything around you has the impact of making you feel like an infant again. You know what you want to say but can't understand how to express the simplest of concepts. Using a microwave or washing machine becomes a feat of mental agility as you memorize the purpose of each switch rather than read the labels. Following directions or finding an address becomes near impossible.

This is why it is important to set realistic targets.

You may be tempted to start to learn kanji (the pictorial alphabet). This is actually a lot of fun and very rewarding (and makes getting around much easier), but as with spoken language, set yourself reasonable goals. Focus on the words that will help your daily life (numbers, hot, cold, day, month, year, large, small etc) until you have spare time to develop more.

The interesting thing about kanji is that each character can have a different pronunciation depending on the context. This leads to the odd effect that, although literacy rates in Japan are essentially 100%, most people cannot read the daily newspaper out loud. This is an important difference obviously to English and would be hard to imagine in that context.

There are four written alphabets in use in Japan:

Kanji （漢字） uses pictorial characters that are a mix of pictograms and ideograms. There are 1,945 standard kanji that newspapers try to limit themselves to, but in total there are many thousands more included in comprehensive dictionaries. Each character represents a word or meaning in its own right. As kanji originated in China, it is possible for Chinese and Japanese people who cannot speak to each other to simply communicate via writing even though it has been modified over time.

Hiragana （ひらがな） is the curved fluid writing used as modifiers to words (the ending tense for example) and also the first alphabet children learn. As a result it is often recommended that a new foreigner to Japan learn this alphabet first; unfortunately though, they probably won't understand the actual word even though they can read it. Unlike kanji, hiragana is a phonetic alphabet and so words are spelt the way they sound making things easier as your vocabulary develops further down the road.

Katakana （カタカナ） is a simpler, less fluid, phonetic alphabet reserved for Western words and is a direct reflection of hiragana. There appear many origins of katakana including that it was developed for scientific usage first or even that it was developed for the exclusive use of women. These days though, the important point is that, as it is used almost exclusively for foreign words, you're probably going to understand what it means.

Romaji this is the Roman alphabet, which is used in Japan but sparingly. Some people, especially the older generations, may have difficulty reading romaji but the younger generation is more practiced with their exposure to the Internet.

There are fifty characters in both the hiragana and katakana alphabets and they are direct phonetic copies of each other. Asking a Japanese colleague one time why there needed to be two alphabets representing the same sounds, he responded by asking why we had upper case and lower case letters in the Roman alphabet. I always find one of the pleasures of Japan is that this thought had never occurred to me until it was pointed out by someone else.

The letters in these two alphabets are either vowels, the letter "n" or compound letters containing both a consonant and a vowel. For example, the letter K in English may only be used in Japanese as Ka, Ki, Ku, Ke, Ko. Hence in spoken language, it is somewhat unnatural for a Japanese person to finish a word in anything other than a vowel saying it out loud. This is also the reason why, when written in English, all Japanese words end in a vowel or an "n". In Japanese of course they don't, they finish in the compound final letter of that word.

The most important alphabet you can learn to help yourself in the early days when you arrive is katakana. As mentioned, although there are multiple versions of the origins of katakana, the important thing today is that it's the alphabet reserved for Western words (mostly English but it can be any language for example German is quite common too). The important idea here is that, if you can read it, you probably know what it means. I remember the first time I read "ice cream" on a menu, I ordered it on the spot simply because I could read and understand it, and you will probably be able to figure out the meaning of "supermarketo" which will be written in katakana but you're not going to know what "denki-ya" means, even if you can read it in hiragana or kanji.

Over the years there have been a number of government reviews of replacing kanji altogether however it is such a part of the Japanese psyche that this is very unlikely to happen. Although many of my Japanese friends have exclaimed their frustration about kanji, suggest replacing it to them and you'll quickly find the discussion reversed over how important it is to the culture and how efficient it is to use. Indeed, Twitter has become extremely popular in Japan simply because the one hundred and forty characters are actually one hundred and forty words in Japanese.

Getting around: trains, planes and automobiles

The transport system in Japan is excellent with the one exception of Narita airport which is not only inconveniently located 80 kilometers (50 miles) from the center of Tokyo, also is serviced by a rail system, the Narita Express, which is deliberately restricted to a speed so that it is no faster than the bus service so as not to compete with it. There is a separate rail link to Narita that takes half the time but is only connected to the north east of the city, the opposite side from where most foreigners live and work.

Additionally, Narita, until recently, was the main hub for international flights for Japan whereas Haneda, in downtown Tokyo, was the main hub for domestic flights. This has led to people actually routing themselves through a third country when travelling internationally as flying into Haneda and then transferring by bus or taxi, as there being no dedicated high speed rail link, to Narita. Better to fly via Seoul where there is one airport to navigate instead of an entire city.

The overland and subway systems of the main cities are extremely reliable, clean and safe. The stories of men with white gloves pushing people onto trains are, unfortunately, only too true, although this is only at the main stations and only at rush hour. You'll soon find a better time to travel and a daily commute is quite straightforward. The trains are so reliable that if there is a delay of more than a few minutes, the station will issue a note that people can take to work and present to the boss as the reason they are arriving late that day.

One issue to look out for is that maps inside stations are not necessarily (or ever) oriented with north at the top. This means it can be difficult to match the map on the wall in a station to the one you are carrying and even harder to maintain your bearings above ground.

The main inter-city train routes are now almost all networked with the Shinkansen (bullet) train. These run on dedicated lines and so delays are extremely rare and they are excellent for long journeys with food and drinks being served throughout. To get from central Tokyo to central Osaka, some 500 kilometers (300 miles) to the west, takes a matter of two and half to three hours depending on the service you choose. Tickets for the Shinkansen can be bought up to a few weeks in advance of a journey and changed up to the time of departure.

Driving is also very straight forward. Japan is connected by a network of toll highways and the construction bubble has ensured that there are roads linking almost all towns and villages, no matter their size.

The elevated highway - where does it go?

These days, if you buy a new car, it will most likely arrive with ETC (Electronic Toll Collection) fitted as standard. Once you've set it to your credit card, you're ready to take your first drive on the *shuto* (elevated highway) that runs throughout Tokyo (with equivalents in a number of other major cities including Osaka and Yokohama). Navigation systems have largely taken the pain out of journeying around Japan these days but a little basic understanding isn't going to hurt.

The shuto was originally built in the early 1960s in preparation for the coming 1964 Olympics and to alleviate the rapidly developing traffic crisis on the streets of the capital. The development has been continuous, and since the 1995 Kobe earthquake, a lot of reinforcement has also taken place. There are now over 200 kilometers (120 miles) of highway and tunnels connecting a fast and efficient road system across Greater Tokyo with more still under development.

Entering the shuto you will usually be offered the option of driving through a manual pay toll or the ETC toll barrier. The ETC barriers have a purple "ETC" sign over them where as the manual tolls are green. The first time you try, take it slowly. Normally you can drive up to twenty kilometers per hour (12mph) through them, however, the first time, if your credit card is still not connected or your ETC card is incorrectly fitted you may find you need to execute a rapid emergency stop as the barriers won't raise. At one point, the responsible government ministry revoked a particular type of card due to high levels of fraudulent claims. The revocation came into effect on April 1 that year however not all users had re-registered their cards.

Several thousand barriers were taken out that day across Japan.

Note there is a difference between entering the elevated highways and the main inter-city trunk routes. On the shuto you need to enter in the direction you will be travelling. On the inter-city routes there is typically a single entrance and the road will split in both directions after the toll gate. On these you typically don't need to drive around looking for the correct entrance, they usually go both ways.

In Tokyo the shuto is made up of two concentric circles (more or less) called C1 (the inner loop) and C2 (the outer loop) joined by numbered spokes (think of a bicycle wheel). The numbered routes are the arteries in and out of the city and are made up of seven main highways plus a number of shorter connectors.

Route 1 is the main route to Yokohama,
Route 2 is a feeder route through Meguro and southwest Tokyo,
Route 3 leads to the Tomei, the principle coastal highway to Osaka,
Route 4 leads to the Chuo, a western highway taking an inland route,
Route 5 leads to the Gaikan (north Tokyo orbital),
Route 6 leads to Nikko and north Japan,
Route 7 is the old road to Narita airport.

The shuto, despite its international reputation for interminable traffic jams, is actually usually free and open and a simple, quick way to cross Tokyo. The technique is to avoid the rush hour times when these can become blocked very quickly. There are very good signs on the shuto showing where the traffic problems are and helping you plan the easiest route to your destination.

In addition to rush hour times, it's a good idea to avoid trying to drive out of Tokyo at the beginning of a national holiday weekend or return during the afternoon on a Sunday. For example, a simple journey from Yamanakako at the foot of Mt Fuji returning to Tokyo (about 100kms) can take 90 minutes if you leave before 12.00 noon; or 4-5 hours if you try to leave after 2.00PM. Timing is important and unless you enjoy sitting in traffic, leave the late lunch behind and come back a little earlier and enjoy lunch in one of Tokyo's fine restaurants.

One final piece of advice, if your journey is from central Tokyo and entails driving to the ski areas of Nagano or Niigata, there is a temptation to take a short cut and directly join the Kanetsu by diverting through Nerima. Don't, unless you really enjoy stationary traffic. Take route 5, and go around the Gaikan. It's longer in distance but several hours shorter in time.

Schools for the kids – many great options

There are many excellent international schools in Japan though mainly in and around Tokyo and Yokohama. Western Japan is served through an international school in Kobe however, outside that however, it's fairly limited. There will be an international school in most regions but it may be a long drive everyday so choosing a home location may become an act of compromise.

There are many guidebooks on the international schools and the quality of them are relatively even. Your choice more comes down to what you are considering for the future. The British, German, French and American schools are all first rate but each is designed for children of expatriates who need to maintain a consistent syllabus level for return to their home country. They are not necessarily designed to provide an international approach for the children and have a relatively limited focus on Japan itself.

There are also many more internationally oriented schools as well as an option to choose from. These include Tokyo International School, Yokohama International School and several others where the principle language is English but the emphasis is firmly on "international" rather than any one particular country or background.

Sending your children to a Japanese school is also an option and although this may be difficult at first it's definitely not unheard of. An interesting opportunity arises at the start of the long summer break for the international schools where the Japanese schools are still in term during this time. It's possible to arrange for your children to attend your local Japanese school for a number of weeks until the summer break for the Japanese school starts. The schools are very helpful in arranging this and welcome international children and it provides an interesting insight on the differences of the two teaching systems.

Your name is now reversed - sometimes

Japanese names are presented in the reverse manner to Western names, so family name first and given name second. And there is no such thing as a middle name in Japanese. This seems not to be a problem and just a simple rule to follow but it will affect you directly if you don't nail it at the beginning if your arrival for any period of time.

Think about it this way, if you register your driving license with your family name first and then open a bank account with your first name at the beginning and don't use your middle name in either then your driving license, bank account and passport will be registered to three different people. Not a problem until you have to use the ID of one to support another. Then it's a very, very long conversation.

A simple approach to this is consistency. Always put your family name first. Middle names cause more difficulty though simply because they don't exist in Japan (Japanese people have one family name and one given name only). More than once I've had to return plane tickets or credit card applications because my first and middle name have been combined or truncated to fit the standard form. If you can, use your passport name in full. However it may not fit the boxes so just use the initial for your middle names. At least then you have a start to the explanation.

E-Commerce, the great retail revolution

You can buy literally anything on the Internet in Japan. You can even book a hug at a cuddle bar or order pizza delivery for your evening meal. However, most Japanese websites remain predominantly presented in Japanese and therefore problematic for a non-Japanese reader to navigate.

Rakuten, the most popular e-commerce market place, offers little English on its main site. The individual stores, operated by merchants themselves, are almost always in Japanese predominantly because their target audience remains domestic although this clearly becomes a self fulfilling prophecy if English or alternative languages are not available.

Amazon has adopted an alternative approach whereby menus are available in English along with basic product descriptions available. However, as the focus consumer here is clearly Japanese, there is no comprehensive attempt to translate detailed information and consumer comments.

E-commerce service standards are extremely high in Japan. Same day delivery is considered normal and next day delivery the last resort. Payment can be made by credit card, bank transfer, cash on delivery or even at your local convenience store. Returns are universally accepted for almost any reason and customer service is available twenty-four hours a day (although here also, documentation and help lines would, more often than not, be only in Japanese).

Delivery service is also extremely consumer friendly. If you are out when the first attempt at delivery is made, you will find a note in your mailbox explaining where to call and providing a reference number. Even with basic Japanese it is relatively simple to arrange the time for a follow-up delivery. And the times offered will be provided to within a one to two hour time frame with the latest delivery times often up to midnight.

E-Commerce has revolutionized the simplicity of living in Japan for an entire generation of foreigners. Before the rise of Amazon, buying a book in English was the domain of the speciality stores which were few and far between. Amazon changed everything, first with books and then with music and movies. Today, access to the requisite materials of an international non-Japanese speaker could literally not be easier. Even shipments from overseas are now quick, simple and relatively low cost. E-commerce has changed everything and materially improved the quality of life for the non-native community.

Hanami Festivals and the Sakura Trees

Sakura (cherry trees) are widely planted across many cities in Japan. For fifty weeks in the year they are really not an attractive tree to look at, however towards the end of March and the beginning of April, as the weather starts to improve, they spread beautiful seas of blossom along the sides of roads and through parks.

People will organize *hanami* parties to enjoy the cherry blossom season. Companies send out the more junior staff early in the day to find a good space who then keep it until the evening when colleagues will join. Blankets will be laid out and beer will be on hand. The sakura festivals are rarely organized on a large scale but become oceans of individual parties and spontaneous events that everyone can join in. Take something to sit on, pack some beer and join some friends for a very Japanese day out.

Dogs, cats and other family pets

In general, Japan loves pets. Everywhere you go you will see people walking their dogs or more often than not, carrying them so they don't muddy their feet. Lap dogs, small breeds such as Toy Poodle or Chihuahua are extremely popular as they're more suitable to city life without gardens and large open spaces.

Japan is rabies free and, similar to many countries, now operates a pet passport based quarantine system that, providing the correct procedures are followed, family pets are no longer held for more than a few hours on arrival.

If you decide to buy a pet dog or cat in Japan, be prepared to make a significant investment. A puppy can cost more than a thousand dollars before you start with registration fees, vaccinations and all the other costs associated with owning a family pet. There are of course rescue centers and these will be very grateful if you provide one of their animals a good home and usually are free.

Getting around – you'll need a map

One issue you will notice very quickly is that whenever it becomes necessary to visit someone, whether for a friendly visit or a major business meeting, someone will always be carrying a map. The addressing system itself is responsible for this as the areas of a city are divided into wards such as Shibuya-ku or Chuo-ku ("ku" denoting ward) and the wards are divided into sub-sectioned areas, such as Ginza or Roppongi.

Individual buildings are organized into blocks however they are then identified by the order in which they were initially developed rather than any principle of how they are arranged along a street. Area number 1 is unlikely to be next to area number 2 but may, in all likelihood, be next to area number 23. Hence a map becomes a vital tool in everyday getting around; a taxi driver is highly unlikely to be able to assist if you are without one. So the story goes, once a postman has learnt their route, it's pretty much a job for life.

Do I really need to learn to use chopsticks?

No, but you're making your own life much harder by not trying. Many restaurants will smile at the foreigner who can't use them; some will help by fastening them together with an elastic band to turn them into simple pincers and some will fetch the knife and fork, kept in the kitchen for just such emergencies. Most however will simply look at you and wonder why you can't use the most basic eating implement, something Japanese children have mastered pretty much before they can walk.

If you are still struggling after watching everyone around you succeed, it's probably because you're trying to run before you can walk. Japanese people use chopsticks in many different ways, some harder than others, but it's more a matter of personal preference how people choose to eat, similar to how there are many different ways to hold a knife a fork.

Using chopsticks is simple if you start with one at a time. Take the first chopstick and push it into the V between your thumb and index finger and rest the other end, about a quarter of the way up, on the end of your third finger. Squeeze slightly and this should now be absolutely rock solid and you can bang it off the table without losing grip.

If you do lose grip it's probably because you didn't rest it on the end of your third finger but on the side of it. I don't know why but in about 50% of the cases where you give people an introduction to using chopsticks, it doesn't matter how many times you tell them to rest it on the end of the third finger, they still rest it on the side. Anyway, check and make sure that this chopstick is now fixed.

The second chopstick you then hold like a pen between the thumb, index and middle fingers. The first stays fixed and the second is the one you use to grasp everything. Simple!

One thing to watch out for though is the type of chopsticks you're using. Funnily enough, cheap, disposable wooden chopsticks are very simple to use and you can pick up food very easily. In many restaurants though, you may be given lacquered chopsticks that are rounded towards the point. If you are having difficulty with these don't worry, you're in good company. They are very difficult to use and even my Japanese friends will sometimes give up in frustration.

Crossed Arms vs Crossed Fingers

The universal sign language outside Japan to ask the waiter for the check at the end of a meal is usually thought of as making signing motion in the air or against the palm of your free hand. In Japan, this is like to get you a pen more times than not. The sign language for the check is to cross your two index fingers and, once the waiter has seen you, your bill will quickly arrive (have you ever noticed how Americans pay checks with bills and the British will pay bills with cheques?).

There is a caveat however. Crossing your wrists is the Japanese sign for "no" and crossing your forearms is the sign for "absolutely not". Sticking with crossing the wrists if you want to indicate you don't agree is the safer of the two until you are used to the significance. Crossing your forearms is akin to shouting so to be used sparingly. And crossing your fingers gets the check.

Breaking Point – when you just can't take it

Stress is inherent to any new life whether it is in Japan or in any new country. The way of life you have known is no longer as relevant as it was and seemingly mundane tasks take on a whole new level of complexity as you can no longer read or effortlessly communicate with those around you. You can see very quickly where someone will or will not be able to survive in Japan simply by how they approach the differences from their home country.

Those who approach things by being fascinated, and in many cases, delighted by the differences will have an enjoyable and rewarding time here. Those who think the differences are problematic, or ridiculous, or just plain wrong, will not, on the whole, enjoy themselves and may ultimately return home frustrated before the end of their assignment.

Japan is very fast paced and it was not, with the best will in the world, designed for foreigners. As long as you keep that in mind, you'll be OK. Don't let the stress build (including for a non-working spouse) as it can become overwhelming. I once walked into my department to find someone who had been in Japan for slightly over a year standing in the middle of the floor shouting expletives about what they thought of Japan. The staff obviously didn't take this well however it was so out of character for the individual it was clearly a case where the stress had simply built to a level they could no longer cope with it. If you ever find yourself in this situation and feel the difficulties of living in Japan are becoming overwhelming, ensure you talk to someone. There are very good support groups you can call or more simply find time in an evening to catch up with some friends. Look after yourself, stay calm and go out and rent a karaoke box!

Yes and Yes – only in Japan

There are not too many languages where the same word - hai - can mean "yes" and "I'm sorry, I haven't a clue what you're saying". Watch out for this, the first is clearly said with the tone of a statement where as the latter is said with the tone of a question. When I first arrived in Japan this caused me untold confusion as I thought my pizza had been ordered or the waitress in the restaurant understood my choices. A "hai" with a clear accent at the end is more than likely to be someone saying they don't understand you rather than the person agreeing with what has been said.

Beer Gardens – the pleasure of summer

Beer gardens are a wonderful summer experience across most of Japan. As the temperature rises and the humidity heads towards 100% life can become fairly unendurable at street level. To help you cope with this the Japanese system of Beer Gardens comes as a great relief.

Typical beer gardens will be opened during the summer months on the roofs of department stores across the city. There is usually a fixed price for entry and then it's all you can eat and all you can drink for the evening. As the entry fee is usually around ¥3,000 ~ 4,000 this is a reasonable price for someone who drinks two of three beers and enjoys a cheap and cheerful dinner. For a foreigner capable of dinking five or six beers through an evening and still be relaxed at the end of it, they offer fantastic value for money.

The typical drinks on offer will include soft drinks as well as beer but also a very refreshing summer drink called chu-hi. This could be compared to lemonade with a shot of shochu in the bottom and a lot of ice in the glass. If you've had enough beer and would like to try something different, chu-hi is the perfect summer drink.

Also, chu-hi is relatively unknown by foreigners and so if the beer runs out, you have a good default to turn to. This, in fact, once happened to me at an Australia vs New Zealand rugby match in Tokyo not too many years ago. With 30,000 foreigners in attendance, much to their disbelief, the beer at the stadium actually ran out before the start of the game. Everyone was dry for the entire game, except for me and my friends. We happily drank chu-hi throughout the match as few of the foreigners had heard of this and the stocks remained available into the evening.

Sitting in a beer garden on the roof of a department store, slightly up and out of the heat of the city, I often find it a remarkable contrast to life outside Japan. There may be several hundred people gathered together, everyone drinking and eating, some slumped fast asleep with their friends around them keeping an eye on them to ensure they're ok and I wonder whether this could ever be replicated in the West. There's no aggression, everyone will be in a very upbeat mood and everyone is very friendly and courteous to all around them. I sometimes think it simply wouldn't be like this in London where there would bound to be a fight at some point and people trying to throw their drunk friends off the top of the building. I may be taking the point a little far but a beer garden is one of the real pleasures of Japan to be enjoyed throughout the summer months.

Can I bring my TV and Stereo? – you can try

The simple answer to this is "possibly". The northern Japan (including Tokyo) power system runs at 50Hz (a legacy of having used a German company to build the network in the nineteenth century) and the western Japan system works on 60Hz (the legacy of using a US company). If your electrical equipment runs at the wrong frequency for where you are going to live, it's simply not going to work. However, you can buy frequency transformers to adjust for this if it becomes a significant issue. This, by the way, was the reason western Japan couldn't supply additional power to northern Japan following the earthquake of 2011. The frequencies were simply not compatible and the transformers required to adjust the power supply in any significant terms don't exist.

Next, the power supply voltage is 100v in Japan so anything from Europe probably won't work. With the US voltage being 120V you should find most devices do work but will be lower power than you are used to, so for example, a hair dryer may operate at a slightly lower temperature than is normal and any lights will be dimmer than you are used to. 220-240V (European standard) devices will probably simply not work at all though and general advice is simply do not plug these in. In this instance it is possible to buy a voltage transformer to adjust for this but they can be bulky and cause electrical interference, a problem for audiophiles.

The next issue is that Japan operates on the NTSC standard for television. If you are coming from a PAL or SECAM country then your TV will not work either unless it is dual format and can switch automatically to NTSC. Similarly with DVD's and DVD players, Japan operates on DVD Region 2, the same as the UK but different from the US (Region 1). UK DVD's will then play on Japanese DVD players but American ones will not. The simplest solution to this now that DVD players are so inexpensive is to buy two, one for your home country region DVD's and one for Japan's Region 2. There are multi-region DVD's available in the stores of Akihabara however these have been chipped ex-factory so the warranty is void and they may be unreliable. For the price of a second DVD player, you will save yourself a lot of frustration by simply having two plugged into your television.

Computers are generally not a problem as most are multi-frequency, multi-voltage these days. However, game consoles that use DVD's will suffer from the same issues that DVD players do, as they are also region coded. There is also the issue you may not want to buy game DVD's in Japan as they are typically monolingual. This isn't a problem some of the time when the games are obvious but can become problematic for the more complex ones when the on-screen instructions are all in kanji. The savior here is Amazon that will ship DVD's and games from most home countries. The other issue is, it's a great way to learn kanji.

iTunes, Netflix and e-reader content are, as of writing, still in the early stages in Japan and you may want to ensure that for at least a time, you maintain an account in your home country to ensure you can still purchase your favorite movies. One day these issues will be resolved but it's not working well at the moment.

Can I legally download movies?

No. As of 2012, downloading copyright material is illegal and punishable by fines and/or a prison sentence in extreme cases. That said, one year subsequent to the introduction of this new law, there is yet to be a single prosecution. Prior to October 2012 it was not illegal to download copyright material but it was illegal to upload it as the focus was on source of supply rather than demand.

The music and entertainment industry successfully lobbied the government for a change in law and, as in many other countries that adopted this strategy, have watched legal sales fall even further as new artists struggle to gain recognition in the market. VPN's are legal in Japan, however this is simply side stepping the issue of being identified downloading copyright material. The actual downloading itself remains illegal whether you are caught or not.

Banking and choosing a bank

If you plan to stay for any period of time you will be in need of a Japan based bank, whether for salaries, expenses or to pay you utility bills in a simple way. Some companies will insist you open a domestic Japanese bank account even if you have a local international bank account. If this happens, just go with the flow, it's less stress and you don't actually need to use it, it's just part of the unchangeable HR process.

When I arrived in Japan in the early 1990s ATMs closed at 6.00PM and stayed closed over the weekends. Luckily the world has changed since then and banking is available 24/7 and even Internet banking in a basic form is available now (I'll come back to this later).

Some banks even offer ATM service in English, though others will offer the "English" option button to bring up a sign that says "This service is not available in English". You have to think someone actually designed that.

As many utility services including electricity, gas, phone don't accept direct debit via foreign banks you may want to consider opening two accounts.

In an international bank the ATMs, branch staff and even the registration forms will be in English. Currently only Citibank offers this service though HSBC has been in to the market twice in twenty years and out both times. Your Citibank card will also work in all main Japanese banks and convenience stores (which also operate 24/7) as well as globally which is useful when you're travelling.

You might want to consider a second account to pay utilities as mentioned, however, be ready for a long investment in time and energy. There is a form for everything and when I arrived I wondered why there were waiting chairs in the bank. Now I think it's normal and am rather glad of them. This is the reason it may not be the best idea to operate from a single Japanese account but it can be done.

Things have changed since I first landed in Japan. With a solid job at a global financial firm behind me and walking into the branch in the same office building, I applied for an account with one of the largest banks in Japan at the time. I was rejected by the manager who told me he wanted to see if I'd still be around in six months. Citibank welcomed me with open arms and I've been there ever since.

Using an ATM is getting easier these days as more are offering English. However in Japanese they're fairly simple. Look for the kanji that looks like a candelabra, press it, put your card in and enter your pin code. Once you've entered the amount look for a green button with two kanji on it. That's the confirm button and you're on your way. If it's not your actual bank there will be a small fee and a screen asking you to confirm it's ok, simply press the same green, two kanji button. At the end, when you can hear cash being counted, there will be a final screen asking if you would like a receipt. Press either and just wait for your money. If everything goes wrong and the machine swallows your card, look for the red emergency button and say "help" when the person comes on-line. They probably won't speak English but will see the problem and sort it out for you.

Internet banking in Japan is, at time of writing (2013) still fairly basic. This is all because of banking laws and nothing to do with technology. You cannot send yen overseas to a yen account by on-line banking but you can send it to a foreign currency account outside Japan. Also, you need to pre-register your destination accounts before you can send it. To do this you can apply on-line for a new destination account but you'll have to wait two to three days for them to mail you the security code. If you need a quick transfer, forget on-line until they improve this and brace yourself for a visit to your local branch.

Making payments – everything by the bank

There are various useful and flexible ways to make payments in Japan but let me start with the caveat that cheques aren't one of them. If you come from a country where cheques are normal, they passed Japan by completely. Even trying to deposit a third party check into your bank account can take several weeks. Bottom line, leave your checkbook at home.

Domestic payments are simple though. You can pay your electricity or phone bill at the local convenience store, you can pay for your Amazon deliveries in cash at the door and bank transfers are also simple (and usually the most common form of payment). You can even make the payment from an ATM machine though in this instance, you will probably need Japanese support.

International payments are a different ball game. Transferring money out of Japan can be extremely cumbersome. If at all possible, use a credit card to make overseas payments, or take a good book with you to the bank if you decide to try the transfer route, you will be there quite some time.

Handkerchiefs and the look of horror

It may seem strange but the simple act of blowing your nose in public can bring looks of shock and horror if you use a handkerchief rather than a tissue (which can be found everywhere across Japan being handed out on the street). The issue is that handkerchiefs here are used for wiping your hands and face on a hot summers day and not for clearing the excesses of a cold. The assumption is that, once you've wiped your nose clean, you'll use the same cloth to wipe your face. And everyone will be too polite to mention it even though no one would ever really consider doing just that.

There is one additional reason not to use your handkerchief to blow your nose. Many public washrooms tend not to have hand towels or a way to dry your hands. This is again where the Japanese handkerchief comes into play and is significantly more elegant than desperately wiping your hands on your trousers.

Drinking and driving – a zero tolerance policy

Japan has introduced a zero tolerance policy to drinking and driving even though it may seem more common than in many countries on the face of it. If you have a glass of beer, leave the car behind. A friend of mine once decided that this particular rule didn't necessarily apply to him. Nine days later they released him from jail.

There is a very good alternative in the *daiko* system. If you drive to a night out and have a few drinks, you can call the daiko service (Japanese only, so you may need a friend to help) and twenty minutes later two men will arrive in a small car. One of them will then drive your car home for you and the other will follow along to pick his colleague up from the destination. The cost is usually slightly less than the price of two taxi fares so it's a little less than if you took a taxi home and then another to collect your car the following day.

How do I switch off that shutter noise?

The simple answer is that you can't. By law, all camera phones must make an audible shutter like noise when a photograph is taken. This is to ensure that people are aware a photo is actually being taken and to help reduce the problem of invasive pictures. There will undoubtedly be Apps available for smartphones to mask this though legally they must make a sound.

The issue is really one of personal privacy. Japan has its fair share of characters attempting to take unwanted pictures and this is one way to help reduce the problem. Unless you have a very good reason to install software to silence the camera it's a good idea to leave it active. The police won't take kindly to it if you're accused of being a stalker on a train as it were.

Medical Support – what do I do if...

Japan has excellent medical facilities to support the foreign community. A quick search of the web will identify both medical practices and physiotherapy clinics that operate in multiple languages in most main cities. As it is somewhat of a niche market the international medical centers can be a little expensive however the costs are accepted by the main international insurance companies.

Separately, Japanese health insurance covers anyone working in Japan on a domestic employment contract. The salary deductions include social insurance and in return, you will receive a green card that needs to be presented when paying for Japan medical services. This card provides a 70% discount on the price of treatment so a good thing to bring along. In the instance you are working on an expatriate off-shore contract, you will not be covered by this scheme (reasonably so as you're not making social insurance contributions) and so its important to ensure your package includes health insurance if this is the case.

At most emergency medical centers in Tokyo there will likely be English speaking staff on hand. As a language German is also common amongst Japanese doctors for legacy reasons. However, once out of the main cities, English disappears quickly so you may need a friend for support.

The names of specific medications differ from country to country. This is generally not a problem until it comes to the issue of allergies. If there is anyone in the family with severe allergies, it will be worth making a note of the name of the offending item in Japanese. Being allergic to Aspirin, I was somewhat surprised the name was unknown in Japan. As I was just about to go under the knife, I have to admit this concerned me somewhat.

Japanese derivatives of medicines tend to be lower dose than foreign ones. A painkiller may vary as much as one western tablet being equivalent to six Japanese tablets so it's always good to confirm the dosage requirements.

Many common medicines from overseas remain unapproved in Japan. This is partly due to the glacial pace of testing but also a good old-fashioned form of non-tariff barrier. The contraceptive pill has only been approved in the last decade after forty years of use in the West though interestingly Viagra took mere months before it was cleared for the market. The powers that be obviously see some issues as higher priority than others.

Bicycle Laws - more honored in the breach

The humble bicycle is legally classified as a light vehicle in Japan. However the associated laws are, as the saying goes, "more honored in the breach than the observance". People generally ride on the sidewalk, or if on the road, head on into traffic. Helmets are rare although mandatory for children and the limit is one passenger although two children strapped front and back is a common sight. If you buy a bicycle or bring one to Japan, register it with the police. If you are stopped they will check it's not stolen and if you're not registered, you're at the beginning of a lot of paperwork.

And now for something completely different

In 1998, the city of Nagano was host to the Winter Olympics and proceeded to develop first-rate winter sports facilities across the prefecture. In addition the shinkansen was extended from Tokyo to Nagano cutting the journey time from around five hours to a little over two and a half.

One of the facilities was the bobsleigh run which hosts not only bobsleigh, but also luge and skeleton. Unbelievably, skeleton, where you are facedown and head first, is actually considered the safest of the three disciplines. If you fall off a skeleton sled you're only a few inches from the ice and the two of you will travel as a pair together to the end. Fall off a luge and you may become airborne and that can get unpleasant.

This is where it gets awesome. Twice a year, the track is opened for public days. For ¥2,000 you can register and actually race down the Olympic track reaching speeds of over 50mph. Everything, registration to safety instruction, is in Japanese so you may need some help but you will merely be a passenger on the sled and no previous experience is required. The first run, to let you get used to the idea, is from one third from the bottom. They push you off and a team is waiting to catch you at the finish line. Then it's one third from the top and you really feel the speed.

All safety gear is provided though the helmets tend to be for a slightly smaller size than I was comfortable with and the feeling is a little like Darth Vader as you breath in and out. Then one push and you're off. The finish line is a long straight incline and almost everyone finishes at around the same point where the team is waiting for you. However, as a foreigner, you may have a bit more gravity on your side than the system was designed for. I went through the finishing trap doing about 30mph and the crew had to sprint up the ice to catch me before I started coming back down again. What a day though, you come away with your official time listings as a souvenir and a huge smile on your face.

Where, and where not, to buy an umbrella

It rains in Japan. Quite a lot. And this means you are going to need an umbrella. I, and a number of my friends have confirmed they too made this mistake, went to the local department store to buy an umbrella when I first arrived. ¥5,000 ($50) later I had purchased the cheapest umbrella available but was somewhat in shock as to the price I'd paid.

If you need an umbrella, go either to the station or your local convenience store. They will have a nice selection of plastic umbrellas for around ¥500, 10% of the price I originally paid. This also makes good sense from the perspective that umbrellas tend to be seen as public property in Japan and although you have conscientiously left your umbrella outside the restaurant, that's no guarantee it will be there when you leave.

Don't worry, your TV does work in English

Since the late 1980s, all TVs over 24 inch in Japan have been bilingual which is obviously good news if you're just arriving. However, the default language is Japanese and not all programs are in English either. If you're watching on a terrestrial channel, eg BBC or CNN, and the audio is in Japanese, look for a button on the remote control with four kanji on the label and try that. Otherwise work at random. There will be English somewhere. It has to be asked though, why is the button to convert from Japanese to English labeled in Japanese rather than English? Never understood this one.

If you are watching satellite or cable TV then it's slightly different. The bilingual button is on the satellite remote rather than the TV one and each remote is slightly different. Some you need to use the buttons on the remote, some you need to scroll through the menu. Ask a Japanese friend is the best advice I can provide but remember they probably won't have done it before so it may take them some time too!

One caveat, it is not uncommon that when you change channel the language setting defaults back to Japanese. Apparently this is the number one complaint received by Sky Perfect (*Skapa* in Japanese, the only satellite service provider) according to a friend of mine who worked there. Solution - really learn the correct button sequence quickly.

Areas to live - the good and not so good ideas

If you're coming to Japan as a traveller or a young English teacher, have a great time. Wherever you live, you'll have fun and a great experience. The key issues to consider are easy transit routes to where you work, and just as importantly where you play. Japan is going to be an incredible time for you, enjoy it.

However, if you're coming to Japan as an expat you obviously need to consider a few other issues. An easy commute to work and home from the inevitable (and highly enjoyable) business dinner, access to schools and ease of living. In Tokyo, as in most cities, there are areas that are, probably for historical reasons, well established for supporting foreigners and some which just aren't designed that way.

If you choose your home (because that's what it should be) it's a good idea to focus on the areas that are accustomed to having foreigners around. This is more important than at first sight as it will remove just that little bit of extra stress from your daily life especially if you have a non-working spouse (more expatriations fail due to the spouse being unsettled than for any other reason).

Unless you have a friendly foreigner in the office, probably no one is going to mention this as it simply won't occur to them. That includes not just your Japanese colleagues but also the real estate agents even if they are used to foreigners. In Tokyo, the best established areas to help you make a success of your time in Japan are on and around the Yamanote Line (the loop line that runs around the city) between about seven and nine on the clock dial (Meguro to Yoyogi) and then, from these two points, in a triangle through to the center, around Akasaka.

If you are completely new to Japan then this is your best starting ground. Outside Tokyo, if you can't find that friendly foreigner, ask the agent where the other foreigners live and start in that direction. When I first arrived in Japan my Japanese manager recommended a particular area which when I visited I found was over an hour north of the city.

He'd recommended it not to be difficult but because this was the typical area that Japanese would aspire to live. I found that friendly foreigner and ended up in the center of town. If I think about it today, if I'd accepted the first recommendation I probably wouldn't have survived in Japan more than a few months with a very long commute each day and no one to relax with in the evenings, nothing I recognized in the stores and no one I could ask for help. Make sure your life outside the office is as low-stress as possible, it'll make your whole experience so much more rewarding.

Getting a driving license

Obtaining a license in Japan is actually relatively straightforward. Many countries have reciprocal arrangements with Japan and so you simply go to the driving center, take the eye test, pay the fee and you'll be issued with a new license. Your first one will be blue and valid for three years. If you maintain two clean blue licenses (ie no penalties for any reason) you'll be issued with a gold license which then only needs to be replaced every five years. The advantage of a gold license is the police tend to put more weight on your version of events in the instance of an accident.

There is a problem for anyone from America though. As these licenses are issued by the state and not the national government, there is no reciprocal arrangement. I'm afraid anyone with a US license will have to take the test.

There are two ways to do this.

1) go to the national test center and try there, in Japanese; or

2) go to one of the registered driving schools, pay a fee, and take your test there in English.

Your call.

Buying a car

Japan, for all its reputation for a bumper-to-bumper, gridlocked country that you can't get around on four wheels, is actually very pleasant for driving. Other drivers tend to be polite and courteous and there are significantly less cars on the road today than in 1990 so the gridlock is, to all intents and purposes, a thing of the past.

You don't actually need a car in the major cities as the transport network is so efficient, however if you have kids or just prefer driving, getting a car is simple. The one thing you need though is a police certificate showing that you have an off-road parking space. This might seem strange but with the narrow streets of Tokyo, the last thing you need is having people park-up on the side, blocking the road even more than usual, overnight.

One last point, before you invest in a brand new car, it is usually worth taking a look at used options. The quality of used cars in Japan is almost better than new vehicles outside the country. People are scrupulous about maintaining vehicles and you may find yourself just as happy and a fair bit richer than if you automatically go for a new one.

Why buy socks if you lose your wallet?

If you lose your wallet in Japan, the first place to visit is the local *koban* (police box), near to where you think you may have lost it. This isn't to report it stolen but rather to reclaim it, as this is where it'll be. Lost property in Japan, especially something of value is almost always returned to the police who will look after it for a period of time until claimed by the owner (mobile phones are automatically returned to the service provider by the police if you happen to have lost yours though).

There is, however, a polite quid pro quo for this characteristic of neighborly behavior in that the owner is honor bound to donate 10% of the value of the lost item to the finder. This is an important element of the process and, although there is nothing legally binding, it is recognized as the accepted honorable course of action.

The problem arises if there was no actual money in the wallet but simply credit cards and maybe a driving license. In this instance there is no value of 10% however the finder has still performed a service. A simple solution to this is to provide a nominal gift such as a pair of socks or a box of cookies. It may not be the same as 10% but you will have participated in a quaintly unspoken custom of Japanese society.

Going to the bathroom – all those buttons!

Japanese toilets are confusing. There are enough buttons to fly an airplane, for washing, drying, flushing (in at least two distinct modes) and even to provide a faux flush to cover one's modesty.

There is the old joke in Japan of the foreigner, having relieved themselves in the bathroom and not finding a handle to push, is confronted by a panel containing the array of buttons. Pressing one they quickly realize they've activated the bidet rather than the flush and water is spraying everywhere. This would be funnier for me if I wasn't one of the foreigners who had actually done this. Seeing the washlet arm extending I quickly closed the lid only to be soaked from the knees down as the water fired up and out in all directions. Had it not been at a friend's dinner party that may have helped too.

Before pressing any buttons, it's always a good idea to find the cancel button for when things start to go wrong. It will be the one with the red square on it. This is your button of last resort. Outside this, unless you really know what you're doing, simply stick to the one that looks like a man standing with his arms outstretched. Your knees will be a lot drier if you do.

The etiquette of toilet slippers

In many places in Japan, hotels, restaurants, gyms and the such like, there will always be a convenient pair of slippers, neatly arranged, just inside the washroom door. As it is normal to have removed your shoes when entering many places, there are always normal slippers available for you to walk around in. The pair of toilet slippers are to change into when you find yourself in the need. The only problem is having to remember to change back again when you come out. It causes huge hilarity amongst your Japanese hosts when you walk back into the party sporting the latest line of footwear with a large letter "T" on the front.

Can I go to the beach any time I like?

Several months after I first arrived in Japan I was in one of my weekly Japanese lessons and my teacher asked me to explain what I had done the previous weekend. I'd actually had a very enjoyable day out, going to the beach with some friends and generally having a very relaxing and lazy time. Interestingly the beaches were almost completely deserted despite the fine weather.

When I explained where I had been to my teacher though, she frowned and said that it wasn't possible and maybe I was referring to the weekend before. I didn't understand at all until she produced a calendar and proceeded to show me that the previous weekend had been September 1st and that people don't go to the beach after the end of August. Luckily I, and my friends, had been unaware of this and so very much enjoyed our time.

This is an interesting example of how the calendar can dominate some aspects of daily life. Irrespective of the weather or temperature, come May 1, air conditioning is switched on on the subway trains and come October 1, it's switched off. Given that the weather can remain cool into late May and hot into late October, this can lead to some very uncomfortable travel at times.

Outfitting – cheaper if you don't like curtains

Renting an unfurnished apartment is relatively straightforward in Tokyo. Outfitting is another matter. The first time I did this was an unmitigated disaster. I was assigned a secretary from the office to help me out shopping for the necessary furniture and having just arrived in Japan I had no idea what I needed or where to get it. One thing I needed immediately was somewhere to hang suits and shirts etc except there were no wardrobes in the apartment. There were built in closets however these seemed more designed for storing futons than hanging jackets. So, off we went into the city to buy a wardrobe. We soon found them, and, this being the days before Ikea, they were incredibly expensive. I had no choice though, I had to hang my clothes somewhere. So I bit the bullet and the secretary arranged for delivery the following day. The wardrobe duly arrived and my clothes were neatly hung. It was only the following day in the office as I was complaining as to the cost of wardrobes in Japan, one of my coworkers looked at me as asked why I hadn't just bought a cheap pole for the built in wardrobe like everyone else!

Obviously there was a very good reason for this. I didn't know you could buy a pole. And to the secretary, I'd said I wanted a wardrobe so she dutifully found me a wardrobe and I was out something in the order of $1,000 (¥100,000). My own fault, again, I'd complicated things by asking for a wardrobe instead of saying I needed to hang things. The moral of this is, *if it looks ridiculously hard, there probably is a simpler solution*, it's just not the one you're expecting.

Three extremely expensive items in Japan are mirrors, curtains and light fittings. These can easily cost more than your new TV and stereo. Tip: if you need to fit the house with curtains, try to get the measurements and have them sent from overseas, it'll probably save you half the price. Light fittings too tend to be discarded when people move out of an accommodation. You might, as a generous thought, have left your light fittings in your house as you move back to your home country. Check two days after you move out though and you'll find they've all been taken out and thrown away.

I once asked why this was, especially given how expensive they are, why not leave them for the next person. A colleague pointed out that the next people might not like them. True, but you could at least give them the choice and save them a tidy sum in the process.

Anyway, when you move into an apartment, expect to have to fit it out with curtains and light fittings. It's probably going to be that way. There are many high quality and budget price furniture stores around these days and Ikea now has several stores across the country so if you're fitting a new place out, there are now many options at all prices. Enjoy!

Taking a Taxi – and don't panic the driver

Taxis are everywhere in the major cities across Japan and usually just a short phone call away outside the cities. In the center of Tokyo, sometimes you'll see the queues going as far as the eye can see and often two or three deep. Unless it's raining in which case you usually can't find a taxi for love nor money.

Hailing a taxi is simple. Make sure the light on the roof is on and the sign in the windshield is red then simply put your arm up and wait for the taxi to stop. In my early days in Japan there used to be stories of taxi drivers seeing a foreigner and driving on as quickly as they could but that really is a relic of the past. If a driver goes past you today it'll be because he's booked for another fare or he's finished his shift. You can tell by the sign in the window but if this is early days in Japan you probably can't read the kanji yet.

As with everything else, taxis have rules. First, don't touch the door. The driver will open the door for you from the inside and invite you in. Then, what ever you do, don't close the door. If you do, you're actually slamming the driver's fingers into the floor of the taxi where he's holding the leaver to close it

173

for you. That mastered, and remembering you only ever enter a tax through the passenger side, you're on your way. As mentioned elsewhere, addresses aren't generally used in Japan so unless you know where you're going, you'll need a map. This is especially important as there is no driver qualification process in Japan so the driver may have arrived from a completely different city the day before and may not know where you are going at all. The combination of a driver who is new to the city and also doesn't believe foreigners can speak Japanese can lead to some very entertaining journeys.

When you arrive at your destination you pay inside the taxi, do not get out or the driver will probably think you're trying to make a run for it. The meter will show the amount and there may be additional tolls if you've taken a highway for example but everything should be easy to settle. Credit cards are common these days as are a number of contact payment systems (Eddy, Suica etc) but mostly fares are settled in cash and the driver will provide a receipt (*receito*).

Always accept the receipt, even if you have absolutely no need of it. On the receipt is the identification number of the taxi and the phone number of the taxi's lost and found. If you leave a bag or an umbrella, as long as you have the receipt, you'll be reunited in no time at all. If you're quick, then usually the driver will actually bring your belongings to where he dropped you off and save you the trouble of having to have them delivered. And he will most likely smile and apologize for the inconvenience you've suffered.

There are a number of taxi companies in each major city. Their fees are usually governed by local ordinance and so you'll find all taxis have a fixed minimum charge (usually around $6-7) and then the fee is charged by a combination of distance and time. Generally though, taxis are considered expensive in Japan compared to the rest of the world but where else can you put your hand out at 3.00am and get a ride to the airport.

Except for the minivans, taxis are only licensed for four passengers (three in the back, one in the front). Don't fall for the front seat unless you can avoid it, as it's by far the smallest in the car. Often you may be shown to the front seat out of courtesy if you are the senior person in the group, but you'll only do a front seat once if you can avoid it.

One final thing about taxis; you don't tip. If you try to you'll cause chaos, as the driver will try to return the excess to you. I've even seen a friend chased down the street by a driver trying to return a few hundred yen. It's actually more than just taxi company corporate policy though and more to do with national characteristics. From the driver's perspective he is trying to provide the best possible service. A tip suggests you received better service than you expected and therefore you weren't expecting perfect service in the first place. This is a little inconsiderate to the driver if you consider it from his perspective and hence no tipping. The driver tried to provide perfect service and you recognize that. Everyone's happy. Of course it means you are limited on showing your displeasure when the service is rubbish.

A good memory – a pre-requisite to being polite

A very interesting part of Japanese etiquette is to always say thank you for something that has happened in the past. If you had coffee out with a friend in town, the chances are next time you see them they'll thank you for it, irrespective of how much they thanked you at the time. The only issue is this may relate to something recent and significant or it could relate to something a long time ago and quite modest. If you can, it is a good habit to get into just to remember what happened last time you saw someone and be able to make some small comment. The effort will be appreciated.

I read many years ago a book that pointed out you really need a good memory to be polite in Japan and it's absolutely right.

Entertaining at Home – the pros and cons

As a rule, Japanese rarely entertain at home. If you are invited to someone's house or apartment for lunch or dinner, recognize it for what it is, a big deal! Although a generalization, Japanese tend to live in smaller apartments than people are used to in the

West and a garden in Tokyo would be almost unthinkable.

As a result, apartments tend to be viewed more as a place for convenience, somewhere to stay and to store everything but rarely as a place to bring friends to for a social event. Some of my most endearing memories though have been when I've been invited to a friend's house, the shabu shabu was brought out, as was an unusually a large bottle of sake, which we'd proceed to demolish through a very enjoyable evening.

This does raise an issue to be sensitive to as a foreigner coming to Japan. For a senior manager, married with kids it's expected that a corporate living allowance will provide for a comfortable standard of living and there will be no problems. Enjoy inviting friends around and have a wonderful time.

If though, you're more junior and arriving in Japan for the first time, try to be conscious that your colleagues at work probably don't enjoy the same living conditions you do. It's something to be sensitive to and avoid leaving those awkward moments in the office on the Monday morning when everyone is suddenly looking at you in a slightly different way. Sometimes it's best to abandon your old home country hospitality and go with the flow, find an Izakaya in the town and meet your friends there. Your night will be just as much fun and you don't need to clean up afterwards as a bonus.

Your single largest cost as a new arrival in Japan

If this is your first expatriation then you are about to experience an interesting problem. If you've lived outside your home country before then you'll already have experienced this but maybe not to the extent of Japan.

The biggest cost you are going to experience, on a day to day basis, is the one of not knowing what a cost should be. None of your home reference points are meaningful anymore. Yes, ¥10,000 ($100) for a melon can be recognized as expensive but is ¥2,000 ($20)? The answer is maybe. If the shop next door is selling them for $10 then $20 is too much. Your issue is you won't know that the shop next door is selling them at half the price as you no longer have a reference point to tell you $20 is expensive.

There is no price gauging or re-marking for foreigners in Japan. Everyone is treated just the same, the difference being, if you are local you know which store is the expensive one and which one is the cheaper one.

The reason they can co-exist is that often the service is different. The supermarkets provide very competitive pricing whereas the local fruit stand may be more expensive but maybe the owner is happy to talk to you about the produce and how the season is going etc. People like different options, your issue is you don't know this.

I first realized this when I met my (to be) wife in Japan. Suddenly my cost of living halved and I had spare cash to do different things with. We weren't shopping in different areas, just going to different stores. My wife naturally knew what was a high and low price and she could help me through this process. I'd actually been careful to avoid the foreign stores so was surprised at the difference a little knowledge brought to the weekly budget when only comparing the Japanese stores.

Visiting the Onsen – strip off and jump in

The *onsen* is an integral part of Japanese culture and to be enjoyed across the country wherever you go. Depending on your home country, the idea of bathing with other people, be they friends or complete strangers, may be normal or may be totally alien to you. In Japan, it's everyone in together (though usually men and women separately but not necessarily always) and there's no better way to relax whether after a hard day's work or an afternoon on the ski slopes.

The origins of onsens are the geothermal pools and rivers that crisscross the country. People would use them as a communal bath though these days they are more considered an element of the leisure industry than a public service (though *sentos*, a basic style bath house, still exist in many areas of towns and cities for those who don't have a bath at home).

Soon after the Meiji restoration, an Englishman riding with his Japanese guide famously came across a group of women bathing at the side of the road in a warm river. He asked his guide if it wasn't considered impolite to be naked in public and bathe near a highway. The guide replied no, but it was considered impolite to watch.

Onsens are simply a hot bath, sometimes indoors, sometimes out, where you can sit in piping hot natural spring water to sooth away the aches and pains of the day. Outdoor onsens are especially wonderful when it's snowing, nothing like being neck deep in hot water with snowflakes coming down.

These days most onsens are single sex although this is more relating to post war American values than Japanese traditional ones. Even so, there are the obligatory "do's" and "don't" when you visit one.

Your onsen kit, the essential requirements you should take with you include a change of clothes for afterwards, a towel to dry yourself and a small "modesty" towel to cover your, well, modesty. Nothing else required. An onsen, like a Swedish sauna, is au naturel.

Note the men's and women's baths will have a kanji indicating which is which. This is your first challenge, as there probably won't be English to help you out and once you're in and your clothes are neatly stacked and your about to take the plunge it's a little late to find out you've got it wrong! If you can't read kanji and there's no one there to help you, look for the character that has a square with a cross inside it (similar to how a child would draw a window). This is the men's entrance.

Once through the outer door and into the changing room, make sure you take your shoes off before going further. Inside the onsen you'll be walking around in bare feet so the last thing you want is to be standing in mud off someone's boots. Now you are in the changing room, you'll find a rack of baskets where you can undress and leave your clothes. There usually is a lock box for valuables but this is more to protect from foreigners than locals and I have to say I've never used one. Typically you wouldn't take valuables into the onsen anyway.

Once undressed, leave everything behind except for your modesty towel and step through the next door into the onsen proper. Here you'll see a series of seats (usually small wooden stools) around the outside where you can first wash down. The point of an onsen being to relax in the water, you're supposed to be clean before you get in. Wash down at the side, make sure all the soap is off (nothing more embarrassing than leaving a trail of foam in the main pool) and then take the plunge.

Remember the pool is supposed to be for relaxation so sitting and watching the stars is good, butterfly stroke down the center is generally considered not. Japanese people know how to relax properly and can spend hours in the water just enjoying the atmosphere. You'll quickly notice the water isn't just normal hot water but has a mineral taste to it and in some cases you'll be able to smell the sulfur. At a real onsen (of which most are) the water will be piped from deep underground, sometimes a kilometer (0.6 miles) or more and so is considered to have special healing and soothing powers. Whether or not this is the case, it's certainly a wonderful way to relax.

There is no fixed time to spending in the onsen (the word onsen is interchangeable between the actual bath and the hotel or even area you are visiting). Stay until you're happy you've had enough and then you can leave. One more wash before you exit is always a good idea to wash off any slightly oily residue from the water itself. One caveat, if you're not used to hot baths, try not to spend too long in the water the first time, it can lead to dizzy spells and fainting.

You have now participated in one of the most widely enjoyed pastimes in Japan. It's fun to go with friends and you will almost always make new friends when you're in the water. Remember to be considerate of the other people in there though. Don't sit too close to someone you don't know and aim to maintain the peace and quiet of the bath itself.

Alcohol is not usually allowed in the bath itself. This is partially for health reasons as sitting in very hot water and pumping beer into your system is asking for problems but it's more to do with safety of bringing glass into an area where people are there in bare feet. If you bring a can of beer or plastic glasses with you and don't make a big fuss about it, no one is going to be too concerned.

Some onsens will also have signs saying that tattoos are not allowed. If you do have a decorative tattoo you need not worry though. These signs are specifically to avoid yakuza entering the onsen and generally making everyone feel uncomfortable. However, if you do have a tattoo you shouldn't actually ask the staff if it is alright to enter the onsen. This will probably result in them saying no, not because they are concerned that you are a yakuza, but simply because they are following the rule. Take your tattoo and quietly enjoy your bath.

So you've enjoyed your evening onsen and in the morning decide to go down for anther round. You do exactly what you did the night before, strip off, fold your clothes, grab your modesty towel (which should be folded on your head to keep it dry when not in use) and you walk straight into a group of giggling eighty-year old Japanese ladies inviting you to come and join them. This has happened to more than one friend of mine over the years.

The problem was you didn't check the signs as you went in. Typically, the men's and women's baths will be set up slightly differently especially if there's a rotenburo (outside bath) with a different view. Overnight they will have switched the signs around so that people can experience both baths and see all the views (which are often spectacular mountain or sea views). Just remember, always check the sign before you go in. It may just have changed from the night before.

Mixed onsens (konyoku) do still exist although they are a little harder to find these days especially for foreigners but some offer the best of both worlds where you can have both separate sex and mixed baths at one location. This allows everyone to choose which type they would like and for a husband and wife this can be a really nice experience to share together over a small sake and a view of the hills. On the whole, Japan knows a good experience when it sees it.

One final type of onsen is called a "kazokuburo" or family bath. These are slightly smaller baths for just a few people where the family can all enjoy a bath together. To many countries this may be a strange concept but once you get past this it's a wonderful experience if you have young kids, to all have a bath together.

The Power of the Planet

With earthquakes, tsunami, typhoons, volcanoes and snowstorms, Japan is one of the most inundated countries in the world when it comes to natural disasters. As a result, it has developed some of the most comprehensive solutions to ensure the safety of the population.

Japan is situated at the intersection of three tectonic plates making it highly prone to earthquakes and volcanic activity. In fact, Mount Fuji is the marker point where effectively the three plates come together. However, Japan is also prone to typhoons as it is on the western edges of the Pacific Ocean and each year a number will make landfall across the main islands before turning further north and dissipating in the colder waters of the north Pacific towards Russia.

Although tsunami, generated by undersea earthquakes around the coast of Japan are a rare hazard, the east coast of Japan is also exposed to "orphan" tsunami, generated thousands of miles across the Pacific. Tsunami can travel across the ocean and strike with almost undiminished force in a matter of hours and until recent times with modern communications, would arrive with no advanced warning at all.

As a result Japan has also developed some of the most advanced construction codes in the world and if you were to be sheltering from a typhoon and an earthquake struck at the same time, there is probably nowhere safer in the world to be than here. As a result, an element of the high cost of Japan, and one of the reasons why life is more expensive here, is the inherent cost of infrastructure needed to withstand these forces of nature. But when they strike, you'll be glad they are.

This section is designed to explain the nature of some of the natural events that occur in Japan and to provide some advice on what to do if you find yourself in the middle of an earthquake, typhoon etc. *Importantly though, no advice can be a substitute for good, old fashioned, common sense.* Keep calm and think before acting.

Earthquakes

Situated on the ring of fire, Japan has quite a few of these so it's a good idea to understand what's happening and what you should do. Small earthquakes are common and you'll mainly feel them at night when you're settled at home. They're happening during the day as well but you're busy or out and about so don't tend to notice them. The big ones you notice any time of day.

An earthquake occurs when two tectonic plates slip over each other. A tectonic plate is a piece of the earth's crust, similar to the panels on a leather football. The plates naturally move due to the spinning of the earth's core and sometimes become caught on each other and slowly the pressure builds. When this becomes too much the plates will suddenly slip past each other and an earthquake is generated. Either that or it's a giant catfish according to folklore.

When an earthquake begins, the first thing you feel is a sudden jolt. This is the P (primary) wave and is the fastest wave to leave the quake zone. Then there may be a few seconds of quiet and then comes the S (secondary) wave and the shaking really begins. Often an earthquake is over in a matter of a few seconds however the Tohoku earthquake on March 2011 was felt for over five minutes in Tokyo. That said, as this was the largest quake to hit Japan in over a thousand years, you probably don't need to worry about another one of this scale for a while.

If an earthquake is small, look for lights swaying or the reflection in a picture to check it's actually happening. A small quake can lead to a large one so best to know what you're dealing with. A moderate one starts doors rattling and windows shaking in the frames however don't be alarmed as buildings are designed to move with the motion of the waves to avoid damage. If you come to Japan for any period of time you are going to experience this, so don't worry, it's normal.

With current technology, although it is possible to reasonably predict *where* an earthquake will occur, it is not yet possible to predict *when* it will occur. Even the location can be misleading though as the example of Kobe demonstrated when it occurred on an unknown fault line. Even the Tohoku earthquake was unexpected as the area it occurred was not believed to be capable of generating quakes of the magnitude it did.

The result of an earthquake can impact different people in very different ways. If a major event occurs it is a frightening experience and so people will experience high stress not just during the quake but possibly for a period of time afterwards. In the instance you are in a major earthquake, there will be aftershocks as well which can continue for weeks or months however, you need not be completely helpless. There is quite a lot you can do to prepare.

What to do in an earthquake

It is highly likely that you will experience an earthquake you can actually feel when you live in Japan, however it's extremely unlikely that you'll experience a major one with the risk of actual physical damage. Earthquakes though, irrespective of size, can be unnerving especially given the television coverage of collapsed buildings regularly seen from around the world. Stay calm, these are the very, very rare ones.

Firstly, as mentioned, you need to know that Japanese building codes are some of the most rigorous there are, buildings are structurally extremely strong. Brick and stone rarely used as construction materials as these tend to collapse during a violent quake and most buildings are concrete (very strong) or wood (very flexible). Therefore you can relax somewhat and be reassured that, unless you are in a very old building (constructed before 1982), you are going to remain safe from the earthquake itself.

If you do experience a severe earthquake and you are not concerned that the building itself is in danger of collapse, then you should either shelter under a table to protect yourself from falling objects and ceiling panels or stand in a doorway with the door open. Door frames are structurally very strong and therefore offer good protection during an earthquake.

If you are concerned that the building itself is unsound you should leave the building however be extremely careful to look for falling debris first, this is one of the major causes of injury. Once you have safely exited the building stand in clear ground and wait for the shaking to finish. There may be aftershocks so if you need to re-enter the building, do so quickly and ensure you leave your exit route clear.

Japan has a wide sensor network over the entire country that detects earthquakes as they happen and broadcast a warning across the mobile phone network to all Japanese made mobile phones and any others that carry an alarm on them. The warning may only provide a few seconds before the shaking starts though ten seconds is enough time when you need to reach your sleeping children and reassure them it's going to be alright.

In the days following a major earthquake there is the risk of gasoline rationing and panic buying. As soon as practicable, fill your car with fuel and also ensure you have a supply of fresh water. If you feel the need to leave, remember the Shinkansen can take you hundreds of kilometers away from the earthquake zone faster than going to the airport and waiting for a plane.

Most important of all though is not to panic. If you are not sure what to do, follow the lead of the people around you. In hindsight you will be embarrassed with yourself if you did panic in an earthquake. The stories of people running for doors and pushing others out of the way will be talked about for a long time. Keep calm.

Preparing for an earthquake

There are a number of action steps you can take to prepare for an earthquake. However, I would emphasize that, although it is wise to prepare, you shouldn't live waiting for one. If an earthquake happens, it happens, but don't let the concept takeover your life. *The concept is plan for the worst and hope for the best!*

Prepare two Earthquake Kits

An earthquake kit is the bag of useful items you might need immediately after a major earthquake on the assumption your house / apartment is no longer habitable. You should prepare two and store them separately in your house so that if there is a collapse of your building, at least one of the kits may still accessible. The kit should be in a bag that is easy to carry, as you may need to walk out of the area you're in and it should include:

- a basic medical kit;

- desiccated food, enough for two to three days;

- facemasks, the city may be extremely dusty after a major quake;

- drinking water and water purification tablets;

- money, including various notes and coins for vending machines;

- ¥10 coins for the payphone network which will still work;

- light rain gear;

- a change of clothes;

- safety blankets similar to those used by marathon runners. Extremely warm and light;

- don't forget your pets, include essentials for them too;

- optionally, a back up of your family photos.

Get a phone alarm system such as Yurekuru

By law, all Japanese standard mobile phones must have an alert system, linked to the national earthquake sensor net, built into them. However, smartphones often don't have this as they are not manufactured in Japan. Therefore, ensure you download an alarm application such as Yurekuru (Shaking Coming). It's now available in English and easy to set up and you can choose the level of warning you want the alarm to go off at and set your location so the alarm will be tailored to your situation.

The national network sends an alarm signal out as soon as it detects an earthquake. This not only brings the Shinkansen to a safe stop but gives you an advance warning via your mobile phone that an earthquake has occurred and that the shockwaves are coming. In most instances you will have a few seconds only so know what you're going to do with this. As mentioned, ten seconds doesn't seem like a long time but it's enough to get to your kids' bedroom and check they're safe.

Know which phone systems will still work

All communication systems will be severely disrupted by a major earthquake. If you have an Internet connection, any form of Internet communication is likely to still function. Skype, Line, What'sApp etc are the most likely alternative to being able to make a call immediately after an earthquake.

The mobile phone system will cease to function within a few minutes if it survives the earthquake at all. As almost everyone carries a mobile phone the network will become overloaded and the mobile carrier will turn off access to everyone on a rolling basis to allow a small percentage of people to still use the network. After the Tohoku earthquake this situation remained for several days before network availability returned to normal. It's not an issue of structural integrity but more one of too many people trying to use the phone system at the same time.

The local landline phone system is also likely to suffer from over use and may also cease to work for a period of time. However international phone lines may still be operable especially for inbound calls as this runs on a separate network with significantly lower traffic.

The payphone network is independent of the regular landline network and may still work. Phone cards may not work in the instance that the electricity supply has failed but ten yen coins will still work as the power for the phone call is actually drawn from the phone line itself.

Know where you live

Although this may sound obvious, in the instance of a major earthquake the regular transportation systems are likely to be disrupted or completely disabled. If you only ever travel to work by train or subway, ensure you actually know the road route to your home as you may need to walk. If you find yourself in an earthquake and don't know your way home, remember your smartphone may have a mapping or guide App on it such as Google Maps.

Keep comfortable shoes under your desk

After both 9/11 in America and the Tohoku earthquake in northern Japan, the regular transport systems were severely disrupted and millions of people had to walk home, in many cases after having had to walk down several tens of floors if they worked in a high rise building. The walk home may be several kilometers and therefore keeping a comfortable pair of shoes under your desk may be a significant help if you find yourself in this situation.

Turn on the television

NHK will broadcast in both Japanese and English in an emergency situation. This will provide you with both general information and, if you are in a coastal region, with any tsunami warnings. Understanding your situation may be important to making your decision over what to do next such as making preparations to leave, immediately making your way to high ground or simply knowing if the situation is safe.

Expect aftershocks

Aftershocks will happen following a major earthquake. These may be severe and cause damage in their own right. Twenty minutes after the M9.0 shock of March 11, there followed a M7.9 earthquake, one of the largest of the last hundred years in its own right. As the days pass they will be disconcerting and tiring and may continue for a significant period of time after the main earthquake. It is important that you are mentally prepared for this as it can become exhausting. Try turning it into a game and see if you can video each shock. This will allow you to at least focus on something other than the actual shaking itself. And remember, they will pass.

Leave your car with the keys in it

If you are in a city, the roads will hit gridlock within a short space of time. In March 2011 this occurred within forty five minutes in central Tokyo. If you find yourself in standing traffic and have the option to walk, then your best option is probably to leave your car and walk home. The gridlock is likely to last several hours so try to park your car where it isn't blocking the road, leave your car keys in so that it can be moved if necessary and remember where you have left it so you can collect it the next day.

Switch your gas back on

If you find you have no hot water after a major earthquake then what has happened is most likely that your safety switch has been tripped on your gas meter and needs resetting. Find your gas meter, which will be somewhere outside your house or apartment, and look for the red switch. This will just need pressing in. The trip switch is a simple safety system designed to prevent gas fuelled fires after an earthquake but if you don't know about it, you can be stuck with cold water and no heating. When you reset your switch, also look to your neighbors. If theirs is also off, it's neighborly to switch them back on too.

Plan your bedroom for safety

A major earthquake can topple wardrobes, throw objects off shelves and knock pictures off walls. Ensure that there is nothing that can fall on you or injure you if an earthquake starts while you are sleeping and ensure your children's bedrooms are safe too. Additionally, identify the safest place in a room for children to hide in a quake. Adults may find it alright to simply stand in a doorway but children should know specifically where to go to when the shaking starts. It also gives them something to focus on if the worst comes to the worst.

Know the school policy on releasing kids

Schools will explain earthquakes to your children and regularly put them through safety drills. However, each school will have their own policy on whether children will be released to go home or will be kept on school premises until they are collected. Remember that in the instance of a major earthquake it is unlikely you will be able to contact the school and you will not know whether to go home or go to the school. Ensure you know the school policy in advance as this may save you significant time if a major earthquake occurs. Prior to March 2011, not all schools had policies and not all parents were aware of them if they did. All schools now have clear policies but they are not all the same. You need to confirm with the school what the policy is when your children join.

Be aware of the risk of fire

In 1923 approximately 140,000 people were killed by the firestorms that swept across Tokyo following an M7.9 earthquake. Again in 1995, large areas of the city of Kobe, in Western Japan, were razed to the ground by fires set from leaking gas following a M7.3 earthquake. Many cities have been redesigned and reconstructed to prevent firestorms, however there remain areas within many major cities where the risk of fire is known to be high. The principle danger arises when housing is close together and the majority of buildings are wood.

Roofing on old style houses is often heavy tiles designed to resist damage in a typhoon, however in Kobe this sadly led to the collapse of thousands of buildings, effectively pinning the residents under the debris and then be consumed by the ensuing fires. If you live in an area where these is predominantly older, wooden housing, ensure you know the route to your local fire evacuation point and be aware of the potential risks in the instance of an earthquake.

What will happen after a major earthquake?

Immediately after a major earthquake the highway system and rail networks will be closed pending inspection. Major trunk routes through cities will also be closed for use of the emergency services. The mobile phone system will become overloaded and landlines will also fail. Liquefaction, especially in areas built on reclaimed land, may lead to subsidence of buildings and infrastructure such as bridges and elevated highways, adding to the difficulty of transportation. If you are in a coastal region there is also the risk of tsunami. Gasoline will be rationed and may eventual completely disappear as will food and water.

That said, in March 2011, Japan experienced the fourth largest earthquake in recorded history of the world. The phone systems did fail, but were back in a few days and the Internet didn't fail at all. The roads were closed but most highways were open the following day. The train and subway systems were stopped but were running again in a few hours. Even in Tohoku where parts of the Shinkansen lines were completely destroyed, trains were operating within a matter of weeks. Gasoline was rationed and eventually disappeared completely but normal supplies resumed within ten days. Japan really is designed to withstand huge damage and recover faster than any other country in the world.

The power of an earthquake – it depends

Why is Japanese TV reporting a 3+ whereas English TV is reporting an M6.2?

There are multiple ways to measure and report the size and scale of an earthquake but there is a fundamental difference between the Western and Japanese approaches. The M scale (whether Richter or Moment of Magnitude (yes, they are different)) essentially measures the energy released from the earthquake itself and therefore is a single reference point irrespective of where you physically are when the earthquake happens. It measures the quake itself.

The Japanese approach is fundamentally different. On a scale of 1-7, it reports the intensity of shaking at a specific location. If you are close to the quake, the number will be higher than if you're a long distance away. This may seem counter-intuitive at first but is a very practical way to represent what is actually happening. And if you have a friend in an area reporting a 5 or above, give them a call, they may just need your help.

Liquefaction – as storm drains float

One of the results of the tremors brought on by an earthquake is liquefaction. This is when the ground effectively turns to a liquid and water rushes up from below. This isn't a significant immediate threat during the quake as it's a relatively slow process but can lead to major problems afterwards. Not only can buildings subside but also storm drains can actually float up out of the ground (think of a hollow tube floating up from under water).

It was actually liquefaction and not the shaking itself that caused most of the damage to north Tokyo in March 2011. It also closed the main highway to Narita for two weeks, with large sections of the highways damaged and bridges requiring re-enforcing. If you are considering purchasing property in Japan, be aware that many cities have large sections built on reclaimed land. Reclaimed land is especially prone to liquefaction and probably best avoided especially if a significant investment.

Tsunami – what's the problem of a six foot wave

I often hear people asking what's the fuss over a simple two-meter (six foot) wave coming on shore as they've surfed and played in waves like that back home. Isn't it just a big fuss over nothing? Actually, it's not.

The difference is that, as opposed to a normal sea wave, tsunami are, to all intents and purposes, an increase in the actual sea level itself. Compare a wave that is two meters high on the beach, one that we all played in as children, to a tsunami where the sea all the way to the horizon and beyond lifts by two meters. The normal beach wave crashes and is gone, soon to be followed by another. The water of a tsunami keeps coming, the wave from front to back being potentially hundreds of miles and the crash, rather than being over in a few seconds, may continue for twenty minutes or more.

Tsunami travel across deep ocean at the speed of a jet liner and can come onshore at high speed and simply don't stop, in some cases penetrating many kilometers in land.

A tsunami is also not only a water wave. Once onshore they amass immense quantities of debris that will act as battering rams as they surge forward destroying everything in their path. The only realistic way to survive a tsunami is to keep out of the water. Whatever you do, do not go to the beach to watch. Sadly, someone always does, and they pull the body out later. Just don't do it.

Not all tsunami are preceded by a sizable earthquake. It is possible for them to be generated by undersea landslides that cannot be felt or even for the earthquake to have occurred on the other side of the Pacific and still inundate the eastern coastline. Several hours after an M9.5 earthquake in Chile in 1960 a tsunami came onshore in Japan at over ten meters (40 feet) having wiped out Hilo in Hawaii on its way.

However, Japan has a very comprehensive alarm and speaker network which will start to broadcast a warning in the instance of an imminent tsunami. The siren sounds similar to an air raid warning and you will recognize it immediately even if you don't understand the message. Warnings will also be issued on most television stations, being broadcast in both Japanese and English.

If you are in a coastal region, or in-land on a river valley, there is the possibility of experiencing a tsunami. Rivers offer very good guidance for a tsunami and in the instance of the Tohoku disaster, there were many examples of the waves reaching several kilometers inland as they followed the course of the river upstream.

The ultimate height of the tsunami will vary from place to place and will be heavily influenced by the coastal geography. Parts of the coastline of Japan are similar to Norwegian fjords and the cliffs either side constrain the flow of the water and force the wave to continue growing in height as it is squeezed by mountains. Conversely, an open, flat coastline allows the water to spread more widely and the waves will not reach the same height as in a fjord but may travel further in land being unrestricted in their path.

What to do when you hear the tsunami warning

If you hear a tsunami warning, or notice the sea has suddenly pulled back far further than normal, make your way to high ground as quickly as possible. You may find that some of the local population appear unconcerned by warning sirens. This is not your problem, people have different responses to warnings and the Tohoku tsunami showed many people simply responded too late and were lost as the water overtook them.

If there is no high ground near you, make your way up a high concrete building and climb as high as possible. Pedestrian footbridges offer some sanctuary but if you have the choice, a concrete building is the safer. These will most likely withstand the water however wooden buildings tend to be built on lighter foundations and are easily swept away so avoid these unless there is no other option.

Tsunami can strike quickly, in some cases less than a few minutes after the initial earthquake. It's important that you use this time as best you can. Do not wait until you can see the wave itself as this may be too late. If you are in the center of a town or city you may not be aware of the wave until it is almost with you. The water will initially follow rivers and then roads through an urban setting and the front of the wave can literally be around the next corner but will increase in depth very quickly. Even a wave knee deep can make walking extremely difficult and hazardous so try to ensure you stay clear of the water completely.

Get to high ground as soon as you hear the alarm

Many schools and buildings are designated as tsunami evacuation zones and it's always a good idea to know where your local one is and how to access the safety area. The tsunami that hit Tohoku came in at over 12m in many places so you need to be well above the fifth or sixth floors if possible. There's no problem about being too high. Evacuate up!

Abandon your car if stuck

Many reports came in after the Tohoku tsunami of people trapped in their cars and washed away with the wave. I worked as a volunteer helping people finding their cars in the town of Ofunato several weeks after the disaster and these vehicles had simply been picked up and tossed around and flooded from the inside out. If you are in a car and stuck in a traffic jam, you're better getting out and looking for high ground. Don't lose precious time waiting for traffic lights and roads to clear. The front of the wave travels extremely quickly and the situation will only get worse.

Multiple waves

If you are unlucky enough to experience a tsunami remember there may be more than one wave. They're like ripples on a pond but in this instance the pond is the ocean and due to the physics of a tsunami, the ripples can take twenty minutes for a single one to pass. If you are in a safe position do not leave until you are sure there are no further waves to come which may take several hours. There were many reports on March 2011 of people becoming convinced it was simply a false alarm, though the scale of the tremors should have convinced them otherwise, and leaving safety only to be caught as the waters rose moments later.

A telltale sign - the exposed shoreline

One characteristic of a tsunami is that the wave can be preceded by a trough in advance of the crest. The sea appears to drain away and the shoreline is exposed for hundreds of meters. This is a telltale sign of an impending tsunami. If you see this (whether in Japan or on the beach in Phuket) then immediately head to high ground. Do not wait to take photographs or walk on to the exposed coast, you have a matter of a few minutes before the wave will arrive.

Hunkering down in a typhoon

Typhoon season in Japan is typically May to October during which time twenty to thirty typhoons may form, half a dozen of which may make landfall on the main islands. Kyushu and Okinawa take the brunt of this but two or three a year may impact Tokyo directly as well. A typhoon is same as a hurricane or a cyclone by a different name. It is simply the word used for these storms when they're in the Pacific rather than the Atlantic or Indian Oceans. Unlike earthquakes or tsunami, you will have several days warning of an imminent typhoon from the weather forecasts. These show an expected path, though a forecast can never be completely accurate even a few hours in advance.

When a typhoon makes landfall in Japan you have two issues to think about. First flood due to the rains, remember you can always evacuate up. A direct hit from a typhoon is similar to having someone pour a bucket of water over you in a wind tunnel and it is not unusual for twenty centimeters (eight inches) or more of rain to fall within twenty four hours. The second issue is the coastal problem of a storm surge. A typhoon is essentially a straw sucking up the ocean and sea level can rise several meters.

Historically, typhoons have posed a serious threat to life and as recently as 1959 one came on-shore near Mt Fuji and the resulting storm surge claimed the lives of over 5,000 people. With modern forecasting and advance warnings though the risk has been much reduced although each year a number of people are caught out by rising waters or land slides and a few sadly lose their lives. The vast majority of these though hadn't been following basic safety and strayed outside to view swollen rivers or to remove fallen trees whilst the storm was on-going.

Stay inside and you'll be safe. It is important if a typhoon is coming to seek shelter. The biggest danger is from flying debris and so try to stay indoors and away from windows. It is possible that trees can be uprooted however a flying sign is just as dangerous if it were to hit you. Subways are prone to flood in a typhoon and will often be closed and so offer little shelter so you should look elsewhere as quickly as possible.

If a typhoon does make landfall then expect the rail network to close in advance as the trains are made safe against the high winds. The networks will be closed in advance of the path of the on-coming storm and so if you are working in a city center, remember that the rail networks to the south and west will be closed before the networks to the north and east as this is the typical path of the typhoon itself. If you live west then give yourself extra time and leave earlier to get home than if you live away from the typhoon to the north.

In the instance of a typhoon, many companies offer staff the option to leave early. However there is a tendency for no one to want to be the first to be seen to be leaving. At this point, find a friend and leave. No one will remember the next day as everyone will have their own storm stories and the ones most will be discussing will be of the people who stayed too late and were stranded on their way home. And there will be some of those people.

If you find yourself stranded as the train system closes down before you reach home or shelter, make sure to act fast and find somewhere comfortable to wait out the storm. Restaurants and bars will fill very quickly and everyone inside will be in the same situation with no transport home and therefore no incentive to leave their seat either. If your train is stopped, find a restaurant quickly, take a seat and prepare to wait. Better to be seated in a crowded restaurant than standing in the rain at the station.

Although the winds of a typhoon can be extremely strong, the typhoon itself may only be travelling at a relatively slow pace. This speed will define how long the typhoon will take to completely pass by. A fast moving typhoon may be over in a matter of one or two hours however a slow moving one may take half a day to completely pass. It is extremely rare that a typhoon stalls, although not completely unheard of, in which case it can last in an area for even longer.

The upside of a typhoon is it clears the air of pollution and the sunset the day after is likely to be spectacular. You may also notice the sun feels significantly stronger, again due to the clearing of air pollution. The most interesting effect though is called "fox tears" when, due to the super saturated air following the storm, it can actually start to rain from clear blue skies.

Typhoons have another important relevance to Japan. In 1274 and again in 1281, Japan was under threat from the Mongol armies of Kublai Khan. The Mongol Empire was the largest the world had seen, an invincible army that had marched from Asia across Europe. Kublai Khan had now set his sights on conquest of Japan and raised an army of over 140,000 men. However, with the ships lying at anchor off the coast of Japan, a typhoon blew up and destroyed the fleet. The "Divine Wind" or "kamikaze" had delivered Japan from invasion and certain defeat.

Are there Tornados? – rare, but they do happen

Japan, similar to almost all countries anywhere in the world, experiences occasional tornados. However, they are statistically extremely rare and not something to plan for in particular although 2013 has seen an uncharacteristic number. Excluding 2013, there have been three reported tornados and four deaths in Japan in the previous twenty years so really not something to be concerned about.

Tornados are extremely destructive and should you see one, take shelter as quickly as possible. As the main risk is flying debris, you should try to take shelter in a concrete building, stay away from the windows and wait for the tornado to pass. If you find yourself in the open, seek any shelter available that is low to the ground. Streams and narrow river banks offer some protection and sheltering under a bridge can keep you safe.

Tornados are also often accompanied by large hailstones, large enough to break the glass on a car windscreen. If you are in a car, always sit away from the windows and sit under the metal of the roof of the car.

Heavy snowfalls – and the making of snowmen

In the countryside outside the major cities, people in general know how to live with snow. Snowfalls of several meters are not uncommon on the Japan Sea coast or on the northern island of Hokkaido. The main risk here is snow and ice falling from roofs and trees. Be aware of what you are walking under especially when the snow begins to thaw, as snow falling from a building can easily weigh several tons.

The cities of the Pacific coast are an entirely different story, where snowfall is very rare, coming may be once every five years or so, and people are unused to the implications when it does come down. Drivers have little or no experience of driving in snow and seem to expect cars to handle as normal. The biggest danger you will face is cars that are out of control sliding into each other or towards pedestrians. If it snows in the city, avoid the roads.

If you do find yourself driving on a highway or shuto (elevated highway) when a heavy snowfall starts it is important to exit onto normal roads quickly as possible. The highways will close and only cars with snow tires or chains are allowed to continue. Therefore, if you are on the highway when it closes, you will be stranded until the roads have been cleared. Similarly, the exit roads on the shuto are closed in heavy snowfalls as the down ramps become too dangerous to traverse. Again, cars will simply be stranded until the exits can be cleared and made safe.

Sadly, a significant cause of casualties each year appears to be amongst the older generation who decide to climb onto their roofs and attempt to clear the snow from them. Each year there are a number of reports where people doing this have slipped and fallen with tragic consequences to the ground below. If invited to clear snow off a roof you might want to think twice before joining.

What to do if there is a Flood Warning

Sudden downpours or rainfall from a typhoon can create flood issues in Japan. Almost all rivers have flood prevention infrastructure, indeed it is said that there is only one remaining river in Japan without some form of concrete lining, and as a result floods tend to be limited to extreme cases these days. For example, in 2012 a flood warning was issued for the center of Nagoya and impacted over one million people. In this case, as it affected a densely populated urban area, there was no option to evacuate the city but as the warnings explained, you don't need to go out, your best route for escape is to go up. Find a department store with restaurants on the top floors and simply wait it out.

The Summer Heat – not the best to visit Japan

The summer months of July and August can become extremely uncomfortable as the mercury climbs into the high 30s and the humidity approaches 100%. Stepping outside you are instantly soaked in perspiration and the combination becomes debilitating. It may seem peculiar that it is possible to suffer heat stroke in the center of a major city but it remains very possible. The department stores will offer relief with their constant air conditioning but running a house or apartment for twenty four hours a day will become expensive. Constantly drink water to avoid dehydration and be especially careful with young children as they may not realize they are beginning to suffer heat stroke. Heat stroke is a killer and many people succumb to it each year.

Disaster drills – September 1

September 1 each year is National Disaster Drill Rehearsal Day, although it is somewhat shorter to say in Japanese. Police, schools, train stations and many public organizations take part in practicing what to do if Japan experienced a new major disaster. Helicopters fly low over Tokyo and roads are closed at random to simulate the traffic chaos that would ensue.

The drills, although probably ineffectual in actual practice, act as a reminder for the general population and especially for young children to see the emergency services in full action and a few hours of disruption is generally accepted as a good investment.

So how is life in Japan?

This is a very interesting, difficult and personal question and the answer will vary greatly from person to person. Many people start Japan with great enthusiasm and energy only to have this sapped over the months as the difficulties start to outweigh the enjoyment. If you find yourself identifying with this, the good news is you're not alone. It probably happens to half the foreigners who live here (including myself in the early days).

I can tell you that I had severe reservations about the concept when it was first proposed to me that I should transfer to Japan for a time. Eventually it came down to a very simple question though for me. I had friends who were transferring to other more familiar countries such as France, the US or Germany and a number of them were enjoying themselves although a few were missing home and wanting to return. Eventually I thought to myself how would I feel in ten years time if I looked back on myself and hadn't taken the chance. Would I feel nothing or would I look back and always wonder "what if?" That turned the idea into very simple question for me, and the rest is a personal history.

Japan will be different to your previous experiences and even if you've lived overseas before, it shouldn't be assumed there is nothing left to experience. You should expect to live in smaller accommodation than you're used to, don't expect there to be a garden and don't expect to be able to talk to your neighbors.

That said, do expect to meet friendly people willing to help you when you need it, do expect to live in a country where children are safe to travel to school on the train on their own from the age of six or seven and where women can walk home at night without being concerned they're being followed. Do expect things to go wrong and do expect to become very stressed at times but also expect to experience something you'd never see if you stayed at home and do expect your children to become international and never have a concern as they grow about living in one culture or another, they will become part of the international generation.

If you are the type of person who is open to life taking different directions then you will probably enjoy your time in Japan. If you are someone who has to have everything "just the way they like it", make sure you have the chance to visit Japan before you commit to a significant time on the ground because Japan simply doesn't accommodate that. One of my roles working in international companies over the years has been to talk to prospective expatriates, and where appropriate their spouses, as to whether they will be able to settle and become successful here. Usually you can tell almost immediately whether someone will be comfortable simply by the reaction to the first twenty-four hours after landing at Narita. If there are a lot of questions and a smile on their face, it's always a good sign. If there's a lot of statements about what was wrong with the journey into Tokyo, the hotel, the taxi to the office, why can't they speak English and so on, it's usually a sign that the transfer isn't going to be easy and the individual should seriously re-think their commitment.

I made the move to Japan and my family became part of the international generation where Skype is normal and friends live in many different countries and have never looked back. But it's not for everyone. It will ultimately be your own decision but the best advice I can provide is to expect everything to be different, and enjoy those differences.

The final issue to be aware of is that you will not be the same person again. I'm still asked by friends from home how can I live in here. To me it's a question I could never have thought of on my own but something I can't explain. From many years ago, when the question came up, I would simply change the conversation. Everything you are used to will change, and if you're open to that, you will have the time of your life in Japan!

Printed in Great Britain
by Amazon